The Greenheart Way

Working with
Natures Elemental Energies

By

Leslie Hart-Rudd

Introduction

My desire, and hope, is for the information in this book to take you page by page through an awareness and knowledge of a way you may not have considered, or were even aware of. To bring you an understanding, and knowing of a way of life that can help you accept and connect with the energies that created not only you but all life whatever kind it may be. I want to make you aware of the wonderful abilities that you and the life around you possess and share.

This knowing, this way of life is based on, and part of nature. It is rooted in the real world where life and death play equal roles in completing, maintaining and turning the circle of life!

Circle of life

A ray of light
A spec of earth
A breath of air
A drop of dew
A spark of creation

New life
New beginnings
New adventures
New experiences
New dreams

The passing of time
The changes of life
The end of an era
The end of a life

Stillness
Silence
Decay
Darkness

A ray of light

I ask you to read slowly as you go through the pages of this book, to give some thought to the possibilities and options you come across. You may feel inclined to just quickly scan or skip over some bits, but by doing this you can miss a small detail that will help other parts fall into place later in the book.

If you do decide to walk the Greenheart path you will probably be giving more intentional thought to some of your decisions than you had before, always remember that **Decisions** lead to **Actions**, all **Actions** have **Consequences**, and you will become more aware that the **Consequences** of **Your Actions** will be **Your Responsibility**.

We will be looking at some of the possible Decisions, Actions, Consequences, and Responsibilities as we go through the different areas within this book.

The following information is based on what I was initially taught in Greenheart and learnt over the years, I have no formal qualifications in anything I have written in this book (I do not think such a thing exists or is possible) and I cannot be held responsible for your actions and their outcome after reading it. But take it slowly, think about what you are doing and everything should be okay.

Table of Contents

Personal Tools

Rituals and Celebrations

Personal Dedication & Commitment Ritual

Let Us Go a Little Deeper

Back to the Beginning

Words and Actions

Greenheart Origin

Chapter 1

My introduction to the Greenheart way

I grew up in a small village where a lot of the people worked on the three surrounding farms, and because of this I was taught and accepted that nature and its seasons were a part of everyday life and knowledge of the energies that not only created life but continue to sustain all life as we know and understand it. Greenheart is something I grew up with and just accepted as how nature, and life, work.

From an early age, I was made aware of and encouraged to think about nature and all that it is.

I was taught to consider how a small dry seed could lay on what seems dry barren ground until the soil becomes moist and warm, allowing that seed to transform into a living being that can help to feed and shelter the life forms around it. How while it may take what it needs from the earth and the elements it eventually gives back so much more.

I was encouraged to observe and think about how the egg of a small bird, a liquid seed wrapped in a hard shell could change into a living thing before breaking free to experience life as we understand it, how that small being could grow so much in such a short time before spreading its wings and gaining the magic of flight, and how it seems to do all this without any instruction or prior knowledge of what it is about to do.

I was made aware of the different life forms that seem to do the impossible, whether that is to live in the frozen extremes of this planet, swim up a waterfall to reach the area where they were born or use their soft and supple roots to break stone and concrete.

I was taught to watch and learn from all of these different beings. Learn how they do what needs to be done to achieve what they need and not listen to those who have never tried to do it, but tell you that it cannot be done.

I was taught that Good and Evil do not exist within an action, but the intention that drives that action. It is not Evil to kill for food or to protect your family, that is just how nature turns the wheel of life. Evil is found in purposely, knowingly, and intentionally ending the life of something for fun and entertainment, to prove your power over others out of greed, or to bolster a fragile empty personal ego.

I was taught to expect, and accept, setbacks and failure as part of the learning curve of life.

I was taught that he who is afraid to make a mistake makes nothing.

Chapter 2

Keeping my promise

I feel it is because of that simple knowing and understanding I gained from the people who took me under their wing and worked with me at the beginning, that I have always tried to respect nature in all its forms, and keep a promise I made to those at the beginning of my journey, and those I have travelled and worked with since, to fulfil a promise that we all make in Greenheart to pass on our knowledge to others that want to learn.

For many years Greenheart had no name, a name was not necessary, this was, and is, a simple nature-based way of life that was passed from those that knew, to those who wanted to, and were prepared to, put in the time and effort required to learn.

A way of life where nothing was written down for you to study at your leisure, it was, and still is best learnt by listening to those with knowledge and experience who are willing to teach those who are prepared to put in the time and effort to learn.

Sadly, those times have moved on to a point where most people do not grow up with or are aware of nature's energies and seasons, we feel this is through no fault of their own as society no longer seems to encourage people to be aware of nature and the life around them, or take responsibility for their life and their actions.

Today's wasteful, throwaway society promotes the idea that everything is available at all times of the year with no personal responsibility involved.

We in Greenheart also feel losing that connection with nature and its seasons can make it harder for people to understand and accept the wheel of life, and our responsibility and involvement needed to keep the wheel turning smoothly.

But times change and I felt in today's world the best way I could keep my promise was to record that knowledge and information for future reference, my peers and fellow members agreed that I could do this, and also agreed that we could call this nameless path we walk Greenheart because that is how we feel about nature and all it contains.

When I undertook this new way, (written instead of purely verbale) this self-imposed task to pass on our knowledge and way of working, I began with workshops and talks, but in doing this I had to separate the different areas, and after a few years sadly found that most people did not want to spend time on what they see as the "boring bits," those simple and often ignored, but important parts that connect those "interesting" areas together, and keep everything flowing and working as it should.

This is why I am now trying to record all this information in a single book. But the written word has its limitations, it can pass on information, but cannot pass on practical action and knowledge, it cannot compare to actually talking things through where you can ask questions, discuss doubts and fears, then explore and experience different areas as and when you are ready, giving you a known starting point for the journey ahead.

Ideally, we would sit and talk so I could explain possibilities and you could ask questions before actively exploring a topic or area while I could be keeping a watchful eye on you and your inner energy self, but that is not possible within the pages of a book.

Greenheart is not just an alternative to belief systems that make you a third-party attendee of something you cannot see, feel, or have direct personal contact with.

The elements and energies that Greenheart acknowledges and work with existed before man, before dinosaurs, and before the before.

They were at the beginning, shall be at the end, and will be the nucleus of the next beginning.

With Greenheart you are an active part of those elements that created life, and the energies that animate and continue to sustain that life.

Please do not read this book looking for and expecting to find answers to some deep meaningful question. I can only try to make you aware of possibilities you may not have considered, and help you explore things some may not want you to look at or question.

The answers to your questions dwell within yourself, but the information in these pages may help you explore unconsidered possibilities and alternative paths. It is these actions that can help you find those answers.

I want you to learn to believe in yourself, trust your feelings and senses, explore, and develop your abilities, and enjoy the journey of life as it unfolds!

I can tell you how I live my life, but I cannot, and should not, tell you how you should live yours, I can only encourage you to start your journey by accepting the possibility of other possibilities and cautiously exploring what you may find along the way.

Greenheart Basics

Chapter 1

Know yourself

The Greenheart Way is first and foremost an exploration and acceptance of yourself and your abilities, how you interact with and think about nature, and the world around you can, and will, limit and define your progress and benefits from walking this path. For this reason, we will start the journey by looking at your Beliefs, Attitudes & Values.

Do you feel these aspects of yourself are important?

Do you think they could affect your life?

Could they affect your interaction with your friends?

How will they affect what you gain from this book?

It is a combination of these aspects of yourself that helps to shape and define your personality and outlook on life. Do not think of them as three separate traits or parts of your personality just because each may have its own definition and guidelines, as these "separate" traits tend to be a bit grey around the edges and can overlap and affect each other in varying ways.

Let me try and explain, if you believe that with a little help, things will work out for the best, then you have a positive **Attitude**.

If you have a friendly helpful **Attitude**, then it could be said that you place **Value** on friendship and trust, and you **Believe** people and friendship to be an important part of life.

To return to the original questions, I believe that you should not start anything you are not prepared to finish, or at least be honest about why you can't, or won't continue with the project. It may be for practical or financial reasons, or you may have simply got bored and changed your mind, the important thing is to know why you will not finish it. Then give the next project more thought and commitment before deciding to do it.

The same applies to making a promise, or taking a pledge, these things should not be taken lightly unless of course giving your word or making a promise means nothing to you.

Most things in life are like a bank account, what you get out of it depends entirely on what you put in, none more so than the craft. It is this belief that led me to that special wild area that I use, my covenstead.

There is no suitable place at home for me to hold any sort of ritual so I discreetly checked out other possibilities, including buying some land but all to no avail.

Then out walking in the forest one day to clear my thoughts there it was, secluded and off the beaten track.

I know I found it because of my belief that it was there, and my positive attitude towards problems, in fact towards life in general.

Attitude is normally spoken of in a negative way, i.e.; he's got a bit of an attitude! Meaning they are touchy, unsocial etc. I know that is how people see me sometimes, and maybe I am, but in general, I think my attitude is a positive one, although it does tend to reflect the attitude of the person I am dealing with at the time.

I believe that given a little help most problems in life can be resolved. The real problem is that a lot of people are not prepared to either put in the effort, or they have not thought through the consequences of achieving the result they desire.

I once knew a married couple that between them smoked 60-80 cigarettes a day, and then complained they could not afford some of life's little luxuries, pointing out the obvious i.e. the amount they spent on cigarettes, did not make me popular, in fact I was told that I had an attitude towards smokers. I was only trying to help.

Values, are hard as it is a personal choice of things and how you feel about them.

For example; I value life, but only if it has some quality, definition of quality of life? You have to define your own I am afraid.

Trust, this you have to earn, it is not given, I find it is one of the hardest things to build and yet so easily destroyed. I will trust someone completely, but if they break that trust it can never be repaired, we could probably still be friends, but things could never be the same as before.

Truth is a little different, there are times when telling the truth will achieve nothing but pain and sadness, in these circumstances I do not lie but I may be selective, or just bend the truth a little.

Personally, I appreciate the truth from people if it concerns me, as my mother used to say, "Better a thief than a liar, you know where you stand with a thief".

Then again truth is subjective; you have to consider the circumstances under which any 'truth' is perceived.

Honesty isn't just about possessions and ownership, or telling the truth [whatever that may be,] it is about how you interact with and feel about others. It is about your feelings towards yourself; if you cannot be honest with yourself the rest of the world stands no chance.

I think **Values** are just different facets of the same crystal, impossible to separate and yet different. Everyone's view is unique, depending on where they are standing and the amount of light that is shining on them from that crystal at that time.

The definitions and meanings behind these words are difficult to define, my **attitude** is coloured by my **beliefs** and visa-versa, and without **value,** neither would have any substance or credibility and just be empty words.

What I am saying is, only speak the truth to yourself and the people that matter.

Give value to your words and promises, do not say something you do not mean or intend to do.

If you want to get the best out of something, you must be prepared to put your best into doing it. It is no good having a that will-do attitude.

Treat others (especially the energies) the way you would like to be treated.

Chapter 2

Gods and Goddesses

There are no Gods or Goddesses in Greenheart apart from us.

We have nothing to worship, upset, or blame.

We take full responsibility for our life, our actions, and their outcome.

We play this game of life with the cards we are dealt.

We know and accept it is not possible to have another go because we did not like how this go turned out.

It is commonly accepted that all life forms are created from the four elements; Earth, Fire, Air and Water. In Green-heart there is a fifth element, Ether, the spark of life. It does not "give" life, it just makes it possible.

Think of the first four elements as the ingredients to a cake. You can have the best quality materials and top-of-the-range cooking equipment but no cake will appear without the addition of intention and creation. Ether is the spark of creation that supports the possibility and creation of life, and the end-product to take form. It does not "give" or "create" life, it just adds that spark that makes it possible.

All five elements are aspects of the Old Ones. The energy that creates, permeates and sustains the world we live in, they are part of, and required by, all life as we know it to continue on this planet we call Earth, all forms of life are part of the Old Ones, the beginning and end of everything.

A rainbow shows different parts of the light spectrum as colours, different colours are created by and contain different frequencies, and different frequencies are capable of, and do different things. Think of the Old Ones as the rainbow, the Elements as the colours, and Elemental Energies as the frequencies of those different colours.

You cannot have one without the other, they exist and work as a team.

Your challenge/goal is to become a part of that team.

The Old Ones, this is a name we use for the Energy source that is the origin, and destination of everything. This includes the origin of the elements, the planets, and the life upon them.

We do not look upon the Old Ones, Energies and Elements as gods or deities of any form.

The Old Ones did not intentionally, or knowingly create us, and are not responsible for us, our lives or our actions.

The Old ones do not know we exist or care if we

acknowledge them, and they will not "punish us" for ignoring them or doing something wrong.

The Old Ones are the original source and continual flow of energy we call the Wyrd, (we will talk more about the Wyrd later.)

The following piece refers to the Old Ones as IT and explores how IT has been seen, and thought of by many different people and cultures over the years.

IT

It is called many things, but it has no name
It is given many faces, they continue to change
It was at the beginning
Before the beginning came

It asks not for worship.
Temples are just man's dream.
It looks not for gifts.
And penance goes unseen.

It's in myth, lore, and legend.
Some have seen it in a dream
Some dream of its creations
Some acknowledge what they've seen

They've seen the life around them.
They know from whence it came.
They've watched it grow old, and die
Then once more, have life again

They've watched the wheel turning.
Seen the seasons come and go
They've witnessed its creations
As the elements ebb and flow

They've acknowledged its beginnings.
And the life that it begun
They've felt it flowing through their veins
They've learnt to join and be as one

It was at the beginning.
Before the beginning came
It will still be at the beginning
When the beginning comes again

We humans are just a small, fleeting, insignificant life form that has appeared beside or after, many other life forms, but just like everything else in nature, we are still a part of that which we are created from. And so, we draw on and use these elemental energies we are created from to grow, maintain our bodies, and enjoy the life we possess. But unlike many other life forms (as far as we know) we can also intentionally connect with, and draw on this flow of energy for our personal needs, not wants, but needs.

Always remember that it does not matter how nicely you ask, what promises you make, or what you wear and do while asking, they will not do it for you. You must believe in, and be a part of the Nature that surrounds you, the elements that you are created from, and the energies that animate your physical body.

Chapter 3

Understanding the rules

To become a part of something, you have to know and believe in what that something is, understand how it fits together and works, and then put in the time and effort needed to be accepted as a part of it.

So, your first decision must be to find out what it is that you want to be a part of.

A simple way to start is to take yourself to a quiet wooded area. Sit quietly, relax, and become aware of the life around you. Listen to the sound of the birds and animals, listen to the wind in the trees, feel the deep pulse as it travels through the ground, allow these thoughts and sensations to flood your senses, and feel them fill your very being.

Allow them to push any troublesome thoughts up and away.

Relax, and allow yourself to be one with the elemental energies that surround you.

Sit like this for as long as you feel comfortable, try to do this on a regular basis staying a little longer each time.

The first few times may only last a few minutes before you are distracted or feel the need to go, but each time you do this it should last a little longer. It should slowly become easier for you to attain that feeling of oneness, and slowly that connection will become deeper, more revealing, and more enlightening.

Do not try to focus on or connect with anything in particular, just relax and allow yourself to be at one with the sounds and feelings around you. Focusing on something and trying too hard will only hold you back. A tree does not try to grow, it just does.

This simple form of meditation needs mastering before you can cross that line between the two worlds.

Think of a door sitting on that line, a doorway that allows you to travel between the manmade everyday world of ego, manipulation, greed, and society's rules, and into the real world of natural energy, filled with the seasons and the wheel of life. But first, you must acknowledge and be open to that world before you can expect to know and accept your place in it until you eventually connect with its entirety.

Once you accept that you are a part of "Nature," accept the existence of the "Old Ones" and the "Elements," then you will be able to accept that you are not only created from, but are still a part of those all-encompassing energies of creation and life. Then you will be in a place where you can learn how to draw on these energies to enhance your life and help you enjoy it to the fullest.

But everything has a cost, and the Greenheart way of life is no different, this cost is not money or possessions, but responsibility for your actions and their outcome.

Your first Action would be belief in and commitment to your chosen path (Greenheart?)

The Consequences of this Action will include being honest with yourself and those you choose to walk your path with, and it will always be your Responsibility to treat yourself and these people with honesty and respect, the consequences of ignoring this responsibility could include losing that connection you so wanted with nature, being ignored or cast out from those you hold dear, and if you cannot be honest with yourself then you will never achieve your goal.

In Greenheart there are no Gods, Goddesses, or anything else to worship, pay homage to, or placate with gifts.

We work with the old ones, elements, and energies.

We acknowledge their part in creating and maintaining life.

We know we are a part of them and they are a

part of us.

We know we are a part of nature.

We know and accept our place in nature and the wheel of life.

We know that by considering all life forms in our actions and living our life to the full, we are acknowledging and paying homage to the nature we are a part of, and the elements and energies that created and sustain us in the most positive way we can.

Chapter 4

Why should I bother with all of this?

You're now probably thinking; this sounds like hard work, why should I bother following this Greenheart path?

Why can't I just do the bits I like the sound of?

What can I gain from putting in the extra effort?

To a certain degree that depends on what you are looking for.

You must be looking for something or you would not be reading this book.

So, what could you gain from Greenheart?

It may help you find that calm place within yourself that can make you aware of new possibilities, encourage you to explore and develop your personal abilities and skills, or could even help you find and accept the real you.

But if you are looking for power, status, or an ego trip of any kind then Greenheart is not for you.

Let us Start at the Beginning

Chapter 1

Connections

Everything is connected to everything else.

Life on this planet we call Earth is connected to life on all the other planets.

This planet contains parts of other planets (they arrive as meteors and space dust) and the other planets contain parts from Earth thrown into space by volcanoes.

We are only separated by distance and the limitations we create or have been led to believe exist.

The Energies of life, the Old Ones, the World, call it what you will are part of everything on every planet in every system.

It was, and is, the "Big Bang" that started everything we are, and it will be the final-destination of everything that is.

It can help you understand your place in nature, explore and understand yourself and your reactions to situations out of your control, to take a step back from things and look at them with a calm, practical mind.

A little something for you to think about;

If everything is created from, and sustained by energy, and energy cannot be destroyed or created, then the energy that has filled and animated everything that has ever existed in the past is still being used, could the memories and knowledge gained by this energy through these many years still be available?

We say it is, if you know where to look and how to contact it, does this take us into the medium / spiritual area?

We use the energies of trees and plants for better health and to create tinctures and incense, does this take us into herbalism?

We consider and use the natural rhythms of life, along with the lunar and planetary positions for our rituals and celebrations, I am not sure what that makes us.

We use and work with the energy that flows from, and between life forms and planets as a conduit for connection, understanding, and knowledge, I am not sure if this is covered by any modern organization?

We do nothing we do not fully understand and agree with, or feel uncomfortable with, or just because “That’s what it says in the book”

The list could go on, but we do what we do because we can, because it "feels right" and because it works.

But we do accept the responsibility for our actions and their consequences.

In this book I can only try to give you a starting point, an insight into the possibilities of living and working with Greenheart, it may take years of meditation, self-exploration, and practice to gain the experience and knowledge needed to truly benefit from following this path, but they do say that which is hard gained is more enduring.

At its heart, the Greenheart craft is a simple nature-based path where all life forms are interdependent on each other, and as such they are acknowledged and respected for their part in the ever-turning circle of life.

Everything (rock, plant, and animal) are all a part of that ever-turning cycle, but we humans unlike most life forms have a greater ability to modify our surroundings, enabling us to survive on this planet in areas that do not meet our practical needs. But when we change a "hostile environment" to suit our limited human abilities, or to make it "better or more suitable" for our hobbies and leisure pursuits, our "improvements" may be another life forms death sentence, so we should always be aware of, and take responsibility for, the effect this has on other life forms.

It is not possible to go through life without harming something, whether by accident when gardening or building a home, or intentionally when collecting and preparing food (yes that includes both animals and vegetables). You cannot avoid harming other life-forms we share our world with, but you can be aware of your action, minimise the damage, and treat these other life-forms with respect and consideration.

Throughout nature one life must end for another to continue, that is simply the circle of life, and true for all life forms. We are a part of Nature, and as such it is our responsibility to work with, and care for other life forms we come into contact with as much as is practical in today's world.

It is our responsibility to use and enjoy the abilities and gifts we possess, and in so doing enjoy the life we have been given.

But it is also our responsibility to be aware of our actions and their consequences on others.

Chapter 2

The principles we work by

Be committed and true to yourself, your beliefs and those you care about.

Do not make promises to yourself or others that you will not, or cannot keep, let your word be your bond.

When you give your word or make a promise it is being heard and will be remembered not only by those around you but by the inner you. Those around you may stop believing and trusting you, but if you lie to yourself, you are lost and will never reach your goal.

The Energies, Elements and all life are connected as one, this includes; Animal, Mineral, Vegetable and Cosmic.

Energy is the beginning and end of everything, everything is created from, and sustained by the elements and energies.

You are created from, and by, these energies and you may draw on and use them as needed, but do not abuse them by frivolous use or to enhance your ego. They are not malevolent but you may suffer through your own actions.

Think of them as an old well-established tree that you and others rely on for shelter under its branches and food from its fruit, it will not notice if you stop going to it or ignore it, but you would definitely notice if it was no longer there.

We are all part of the same ever-turning circle of life.

The circle of life applies to everything; the only difference is the time taken to turn the wheel.

The life of an insect may last a day, an animal 100 years, a tree 1,000 years and a mountain millions of years, but all have a point of birth and death, and all play their part in the circle of life.

We acknowledge, and work with all forms of life. If we treat them with respect, they may do the same for us.

We all take what we require from the same ever-flowing stream of energy, (we call this the Wyrd)

Think of energy as a stream slowly flowing down a mountain, through open meadows, wild forests and into the sea before rising up into the rain clouds that feed these mountain streams. Now think of all the different life forms that drink from this ever-flowing stream, plants, insects, fish, animals, and humans. Each is so different from the other, and each takes what they need to create and maintain their individuality.

We all originate from and will return to this ever-flowing stream.

When our time is over our physical form will return to the matter it was created from, and the energy that animated that form, that makes us who we are, may return to the pool of energy and be used to animate another life, or it may continue as a new energy-based life-form.

Chapter 3

The energies of life

If you want to use the Energies for your benefit, then you must put in the time and effort.

Do not connect with the energies and expect them to "make things happen" for you. You can draw on the energies to enhance your ability to achieve a positive outcome in what you are doing, but you must put in the time and effort.

They are not your servants, but they will work with you. If you prepare the soil and plant the seeds, they can make the seeds grow.

If you want to be at one with the Energies then do not isolate yourself from them behind an ego screen of any kind.

We acknowledge and work with elemental, nature-based energies that began in a time before time began. They were involved in creating the physical world we live in, but originate in the non-physical world some of us may not be aware off.

To connect with, and be at one with these energies, you must ignore the trappings of the physical world and join them in the natural life they are a part of and helped create.

Think of an old, well-established tree, it stands tall and strong because of the hardships it has endured, not because it has sheltered from the storms and hidden from the elements.

Greenheart works with the elements and energies that we, and everything else came from, remain a part of, and are continually sustained by.

We originate from, and are a part of what we call the Old Ones. This name was not given to create an air of importance, but because it was there at the beginning. It is the origin of the elements and energies, it is the source and sustenance of all life's creations, and it shall be there at the end, but of course, every end is also a new beginning!

Earth and Fire are base Elements; they are the building blocks present in everything from the mass of a planet to the "empty" voids of space, think of them as the physical base for creation and life that Water and Air can attach to.

Air and Water are the energy and movement of life, they fill our lungs and veins, give us strength, and awaken our senses.

Ether does not create or set requirements for life; it merely adds the spark of creation that makes life possible.

A little something to think about; In the chemical composition of things the Earth has 81 of the 90 elements that have also been detected throughout in the stars, and we are part of the Earth.

On this small planet, we call home there is life in the frozen wastes of the poles, the searing heat of the deserts, and the depths of the oceans, the closer you look the more you will find. All this life is created from the same energy that created the universe. We are a part of that all-encompassing energy, just as that is a part of us.

This physical form we call our body has been animated and given the gift of life by the elemental energies. A gift that enables us to make choices, plan our future and to some degree, control our destiny.

The energy that fills and animates us comes from an ever-flowing supply, an inexhaustible re-cycling unit with infinite power.

We are a part of that energy.

We can connect with its totality to enhance our lives and fulfil our dreams.

All this is possible within Greenheart.

When working i.e., creating, and performing a celebration or ritual we (Greenheart) draw from whatever energy source feels the most suitable for our needs.

For example;

Earth can be thought of as strong and reliable as it has an age-old strength that exists within it. but it also contains the relatively fleeting energy of the fast-moving life that dwells upon its surface.

Water may be used to feed and encourage a new venture, or its strength may be used for purification and cleansing.

The gentle breath of a summer breeze can help to carry seeds of hope, and the strong winds of winter can be used to remove those negative thoughts and memories that are holding you back.

The light from a fire can be used to show you what is hiding in the shadows, and the heat can warm the ground for new life or clear the ground from the harmful residue of an old life.

Ether is present in the seeds from what was, the new shoots of what is, to the plans for what will be.

Or the calm strength and gently flowing power of the cosmos may be more suitable for your needs.

Each, and every element, energy, and life form, has something about it that can be woven into the fabric of a celebration or ritual to enhance its meaning and outcome.

But before connecting with the energy of anything, living, past, or elemental, you need to be certain it is the right one to assist you in your desire or need. You should always think about why you are considering doing it, and what you want to achieve from it, and you should never connect with or draw from the energies just for fun or because you want to see if you can.

A word of caution; be very clear and careful about what you ask for or create. Anything you do can and will have a knock-on effect in your / our world in the same way that ripples from a pebble dropped into a pond can disrupt life at the edges.

Think before you act.

Meditation

Chapter 1

A short introduction to a very useful tool

In its simplest form meditation can help you to release stress and relax. But with a little practice, it can be used to separate the physical you with its man-made limitations, from your spiritual / energy core.

It can be used to allow the Physical body to rest safely, while your personal energy / spiritual self becomes consciously active in the realm between the worlds of physical matter and the energies that animate that matter. It allows us to access the Wyrd, a place where time and space are no longer a boundary.

We use meditation to relax and obtain an Altered State of Consciousness. A time when you are able to access, use, and develop parts of your inner self or consciousness that are no longer needed or used in the modern world.

In meditation we see, and use, two distinct levels of contact and interaction, the first will allow you to see, hear, and know things but you remain aware of and connected to your physical body.

The second level could be classed as an out-of-body experience that allows you to leave your physical body and look down upon yourself and your surroundings. To be in another place where you can feel the breeze and smell the flowers in an otherworldly realm or place, to be part of and experience new things, and to help understand not only how they work but where you fit in.

Chapter 2

Guided meditations

Guided meditations are normally better if someone else is telling them while watching over and guiding you during the journey.

If you do not have someone to read it and guide you, then read it a few times to help you remember the details, or read and record it so you can play it back, but however you do it the main thing is to relax and enjoy the journey and experience.

A little tip, do not rush through the journey, allow yourself a little time to explore and experience the different parts of it as you go.

Here is a level one guided meditation for you to do and hopefully give you an insight into the possibilities of using them. Its reason for creation and possible benefits should become clear as the story unfolds.

Warm your hands by the fire.

Make sure your back and hands are supported, and your body is safely settled in its seat, once your body is in a comfortable position have that last little wriggle, and relax.

Allow your body to soften and mould itself into your seat where it is safe and comfortable allowing you to forget all about it for a little while.

Now with your physical self-settled, you turn your senses inwards.

Shift your focus to your breath. As you inhale, feel the air filling your lungs and calming your mind. As you exhale, feel your chest deflate and let go of the day's stresses and worries, releasing them with your breath."

Take a slow, deep, breath, and feel how as the air swells your lungs, it mingles with your blood and penetrates every fibre within you, then once again as you slowly breathe out any tension in your body leaves with the unwanted air.

As you continue to breathe, slowly, calmly, you become aware of your beating heart, you feel it gently beating within your chest, just relax and listen to it for a while as it beats out the rhythm of life.

Feel how your beating heart pushes the blood through your veins, feel how it connects to your very core, releasing a strong, calm energy that seems to well up from deep within you, and with every breath you take, that energy, that sensation grows stronger, and more complete.

That warm calm sensation surges through your body, it floods through your chest and up into your arms, it fills your hands and flows out through your fingers allowing you to feel the air around you.

Feel it flow up into your shoulders, through your neck and carry any cares and worries you have up through your head and out, leaving you peaceful, relaxed, and ready for the journey ahead.

With your physical body safely in its seat, stand and walk towards the open door in front of you.

You stop at the door and look out onto a small autumnal cottage garden that is filled with the fading colours of summer, as you step through the door and out into the garden, the afternoon sun greets you as its weakly shines through a gateway in the hedge that surrounds this garden you have entered.

A pathway leads you from the door and down the garden towards that opening in the hedge.

It is only a small garden and just a few short steps take you to this gateway where you look through the hedge and out onto a small meadow.

This meadow has gently sloping hills on one side, on the other an old wood, this wood is the start of our journey, so stepping through the gap in the hedge, we follow the path across the meadow and into that stand of old autumnal trees.

It is not far to this autumn woodland with its almost leafless trees and find we have entered a silent place that is filled with the knowledge of times both past and yet to come, an ancient place that may hold many secrets for us.

As you follow the path through these silent giants you turn a corner and enter a clearing where a solitary old person sits by a fire, you stop and watch for a while and notice an animal lying close by their side, they know you are there and without looking up they beckon you over to sit beside them and share the warmth of the fire.

You do as they ask and sit beside them warming your hands on the glowing embers.

They do not speak or look at you but take a leather-bound book from within their coat and hand it to you, as you take it the pages fall open, but before you can close it again, they put their hand onto the open page and tell you that whatever it shows, it shows only to you, this page and its contents exist only for your knowledge and use, remember and use it well.

You sit silently by the fire and study this page remembering every detail that it contains, until suddenly they silently reach out, take back the book close it, and return it to their coat, they do not speak but you know it is time to leave, the light from the fire is fading and you must return to the garden.

Walking back through the forest it seems to have become even quieter as the night enters it, even the meadow now stands silent in the evening stillness as you cross, but the return journey always seems shorter and you are soon back at the opening in the hedge, and as you step through you turn and look back, remember this person, the book they hold for you and how to get there, for the knowledge it contains is for your use only and you may return there whenever you wish.

Stepping back through the hedge and into the garden it is only a short walk to the door, walking through the door you cross the room and return to your waiting body.

Now in your own time take a deep breath, open your eyes, stretch your limbs, and return to the here and now.

It is always good to sit and have a drink and something to eat after doing a meditation or ritual, it helps to bring your physical and spiritual selves back together and work as one.

We will refer to meditation many times as we travel through the pages as it is used in many different areas of the path we will be exploring. We will look at a level two meditation a little further into this journey you have started.

Personal Protection

Chapter 1

Is personal protection needed?

We have been looking at ways to connect with and be part of nature, the elements, and energies, and some of you may be thinking is it safe? What about the "dark side," and the "evil energies," do I need protection?

Think of energy as electricity. If you plug in a kettle, you can make a drink, if you plug in an electric chair, you can kill someone. It is not the electricity that is dangerous, but the intention behind its use.

A knife or gun is harmless until the wrong person picks it up. Energy is the same, it is the intention behind its use, energy is not good or bad, it is the intention of the persons controlling it that can cause harm.

The main thing you may need protection from are people with their own agendas, or darkness in their hearts. They may first appear wearing a cloak of glamour that hides their true intentions, they may seem to be an understanding friend who is willing to share your troubles and secrets, but tread slowly as only time will allow you to see the real person.

Watch their deeds and actions more than you listen to their words.

Trust your feelings and gut instinct, take counsel from your old friends, and take time before you allow new friends into your private world.

The act of protecting your personal energy from external, possibly negative or malevolent energies sounds a bit frightening, but all you need to do is understand how things work and believe in yourself, you are much stronger than you realise.

Chapter 2

Is personal protection possible?

If you rely on a protective circle, chant, or any other third-party method to protect you from the "evil, negative energies," could you also be isolating yourself from the positive, helpful energies?

If you use a filter that will only "let in" a specific, known, safe thing, or if you create a protective circle with a door that allows you to only let in those energies/spirits you know and want to deal with, Is that personal protection or isolation?

With your current method (if you have one) are you content to "protect" yourself from possible danger while missing out on many of life's more interesting possibilities? Or are you simply taking an easy option to avoid the work involved in thinking about different methods, and finding the best one for you?

A tree that stands alone in a field has deeper roots and stronger branches than one in the forest because it has faced, and survived, storms, hard times, and attacks from the various thing's life has thrown at it. It has evolved and grown stronger because of those things.

A tree in a forest generally has weaker roots because it has become reliant on the protection of those around it and is more vulnerable to a sudden attack.

A strong belief in, and knowledge of the elements and energies will help create a stronger self with deeper roots.

You can develop that personal protective energy by growing those strong roots of self-knowledge and belief.

It is good to have a companion, a fellow believer to explore and learn with, someone you can trust and feel at ease with, a friend you can trust and who trusts you, but it is not compulsory.

You, as many have before, can do this on your own, a hard/tough path creates a more able and competent traveller.

Always remember that it is better to travel alone than with someone who holds you back with negative actions, thoughts, and comments.

Your personal aura and personal energy are the same thing viewed from different places. The energy that is a personal aura can be expanded and withdrawn depending on what you are doing, and how you feel, happy, sad, frightened etc and can be seen by an empath or even detected by someone with dowsing rods. And the colours within a personal aura can also be seen by an empath or photographed with the right equipment, and just like your energy these colours will vary depending on how you feel and what you are doing.

This colourful aura is seen, and felt, as a "bubble" that surrounds you, a bubble of colourful energy that you are creating and controlling. This energy is a part of and created by you, accept it, own it, and use it. It can become more powerful than any circle, chant, or prayer.

Controlling your personal aura size and strength is fairly simple, but can take a while to master.

To pull it in and make you less noticeable just think small, imagine yourself as a small lonely child sitting quietly in the corner of a room with your legs drawn up and arms folded over them not wanting to be seen.

Feel the lonely solitude of that child, feel and see your aura become dull and grey, and now draw all your senses within yourself until you feel nothing but the clothes you wear and the ground you sit on.

When you master this. It is possible to walk into a crowded room without anyone giving you a second glance.

To expand your aura simply stand tall and proud, fill yourself with happy positive feelings, with love and empathy. Feel how that warm content feeling grows within you until it shines out through your skin creating a colourful casing or bubble around you.

When you learn to expand your personal energy and aura in this way people will acknowledge you as you walk down the street or look as you enter a room.

The size and colour of your aura reflect your mood and feelings, and with practice, you can become aware of your aura size and colours and use them to improve how you feel and react to people and things, and with a little more practice it can become a protective screen that automatically stops negative or harmful energies, intentions, and thoughts from reaching and affecting you.

Achieving this is not really that difficult it just takes time, commitment, and hard work. Work your way through the following and I am sure things will slowly fall into place for you.

Know and accept yourself; everyone has "good" and "bad" bits within them, accept your faults and annoying habits, you do not have to tell anyone about or change them, true friends like and accept you just as you are.

You cannot change your past just accept things happened and you survived and learned from them (hopefully) and look to the future not the past.

Believe in and trust yourself and your feelings.

Do not feel you have to conform. As long as it harms no one, do what feels right for you.

Do not feel you have to explain your beliefs and actions.

Most other people would probably not understand what you do and why, so why waste time trying to explain it to them? As long as it harms no one else, do what feels right for you.

Do not be afraid to stand alone. You are part of the most amazing limitless energy, so why should you worry about standing alone, you are never alone.

Invest the time required in learning how to meditate, then practice until you find it relatively easy to reach that Altered State of Consciousness where the physical and spiritual parts of you can do their own thing.

Now use that meditation to relax, learn how to develop and control your personal energy/aura. Learn how to make it expand, then pull it back in. You can do this by closing your eyes and seeing it grow in your mind's eye until you can feel it touching the things around you.

Allow your aura to expand and open allowing things to contact you, then explore not only what you have come into contact with, but what is trying to contact you and why.

Now draw your energy back in to form a protective boundary or shield before exploring what you felt, how it made you feel, and what it wants from you.

Learn how your feelings and frame of mind can control not only your personal energy but also your aura and its colours.

What do the different colours mean to you?

What colour do you associate with strength, knowledge, fear, love etc, etc?

It can be interesting and useful to look at what others say about the meaning behind the different colours and associations, or how to do different things, but never think they know more than you so you must be wrong. Always remember that if your feelings and their words do not agree, they are talking about their experiences and knowledge based on what they have done, and have no idea who you are, your life experiences so far, or what you are trying to learn and achieve.

Always believe in and trust yourself and your feelings, and do not allow the past to limit your future.

I suggest you start gently and cautiously to begin with, if you do not have someone to do guided meditations with then relax and see what appears when watching passing clouds or the flames of a fire, then slowly progress to having a question or need to meditate on.

Allow your body to relax and see what you see, but do not go in search of something unless you are sure you know what it is, you should always stay in control of the experience.

When you do "sense" something just relax, acknowledge it, and watch it for a while. See if it is aware of you before trying to open a dialogue of any kind. But you must always stay in control of, and own, not only the connection but the ability to close that connection at any time.

Some people think the only energies and spirits out there are of human origin, the energy or spirit that animated or filled a person while they were alive.

But that energy is such a small part of the total array and variation of past life forms and their remaining energies that surround us.

They are simply the easiest to contact and work with because their origins are the same as ours and their energies are some of the most recent and therefore closer to the surface, they are also the ones most people are looking for and expecting to find.

But on a positive note, the more you meditate the easier it gets.

Personal Tools

Chapter 1

Can a personal tool hold energy?

We have no magical tools in Greenheart. The energy we use comes from within ourselves, from nature, we merely draw on it and use it. Magic does not come into it (we will look at "Magic" in a while).

We do have and use a few items that could be thought of as tools, however, none of these holds any power, the power is within us, all they do is help us focus and direct the energy for the desired use.

But when you learn to draw on, build, focus and direct that energy to a positive end result some think of this as magic, but all you are doing is using the tools available.

Let me explain; if you lay a spade in the garden, it will not dig a hole for you, in the same way, these "tools" cannot do "magic" for you.

You need to think about (meditate on) why you want a hole, its location and size.

You need to choose the appropriate tools (spade etc) and learn how to use them.

You will have drawn on and built up, energy at every stage until you finally release that energy through the spade to create that hole you need.

You need to visualise that hole while you are digging to ensure the finished item is exactly what you need.

So, as you see, it is you who must put in the time, effort, and hard work both spiritual and physical, the tools themselves have no power they merely aid you in your chosen task.

But if you use, and work with an item on a regular basis a personal connection is created that allows you to achieve more than would normally be expected. You get to know the feel of an item, every little mark, crease, and bump on its surface. It just slips into the correct position in your hand as you pick it up. It becomes part of you and your energy can be enhanced and magnified as it flows through it. But no, it does not hold or possess any energy of its own.

Chapter 2

Personal tools

Back to the tools used within a group; these are the most commonly used by us and why.

Candle and if used outside, its windproof holder;

A symbol of what you are acknowledging and welcoming, a focal point for your thoughts and actions. In a rite of passage, it can denote the end of something, or the beginning.

Incense and the heatproof dish or holder for the charcoal block the incense is burnt upon.

Smoke and smell are both tangible parts of this world and yet also part of another, and burning the correct incense can create a fragrance that helps to create the right frame of mind to achieve the desired, and required connection needed.

We will look further into Incense a little later in the book.

Cup or Goblet;

This can be used to toast and confirm important statements and stages within a ritual and celebration, or simply to toast the turning of the wheel and old friends that have moved to another realm.

It is not uncommon to have different cups or goblets for different types of rituals or celebrations i.e. seasonal celebrations and a passing.

Herbs;

We use them in cooking, the creation of an incense, and to repel insects.

Important; Herbs or any other item should only be eaten with the guidance of an experienced person.

Mortar and Pestle;

Seldom used as part of a ritual but they can help to create a wide range of items from incense to healing balms. Having a personal set that feels comfortable in your hands allows you to relax more when using it, and that allows you to focus on what you are making and why.

Seasons and Moon phases;

Both can enhance the structure and outcome of a ritual when correctly woven into its creation and wording.

The seasons are used more in long-term life-changing plans, Spring and Summer are natural growing periods and could be used to enhance a new venture or big change in your life, whereas Autumn and Winter are the times to leave the unwanted behind or end a bad habit.

The Moons phases can be used in a similar, but more personal way. A personal commitment and dedication ritual is best done at the early growing / waxing stage of a new moon. This is to encourage, and help the strength of your commitment to grow, as the new moon grows in size and strength so your roots will become deeper and stronger within your path. The waning stage of the moon cycle is best used for something you need to die and fade. With a little planning, they can both be used at the same time, within the same ritual to support and strengthen each other.

It is quite common for individuals within any group to have personal items they carry with them or use for certain things in everyday life i.e. a personal item passed down through the family, or a small meaningful gift from someone special. There are no, or very few rules concerning personal tools/items. If it helps you to move past those human limitations you have been taught to accept and believe, then use it.

A personal item may also help you to relax, focus on, and connect with the energies you are acknowledging, exploring, or working with, and can be included into a ritual's preceding's so long as everyone participating agrees.

Incense;

A few pages back I said we would talk more about incense. Most people think of incense as something to make the room smell nice, which it can, but made and used correctly it can do so much more. It can help you meditate or clear a space of negative feelings. It can help to create the right frame of mind for a ritual, and even enhance the process and outcome of a ritual.

We (Greenheart) create our own incense so that it reflects the feelings and intentions of what it is being created for, and why we are using it. The act of collecting, preparing, and selecting the ingredients gives us the opportunity to connect with the energies of those ingredients and make full use of their abilities.

The following pages will give you an insight into what we use and why, but it is not set in stone, you must go with your instincts when selecting the ingredients and creating an incense.

And remember, one or two pinches of incense is all that is normally used during a celebration or ritual.

Chapter 3

Creating and using incense

The following information is based on what I have been taught in Greenheart and learnt over the years. I have no formal qualifications in anything I have written in this book (I am not sure if such a thing exists)

Always be aware that some plants are, or can be toxic, and some people have allergies.

Before we go any further, please read and remember!

All natural ingredients and creations should be treated with respect and caution, and they should only be used with knowledge of the plants and their possible benefits and dangers.

Important; You must always accept the responsibility for the outcome of your creation and its use.

You may only have good intentions at heart, but it is always possible the end result may not be what you expected or desired.

Making & using incense:

Always start with these simple but important questions;

What are you making the incense for?

What do you want it to do, and why?

How do you intend to use it & where?

If it is to be used inside then use less oil so it creates less smoke, and does the building have smoke alarms?

If spiritual/magical, are others involved?

All involved in any ritual should know why it is being done, and what the desired outcome is

Do any of those who will be there have allergies?

Incense ingredients fall into three main groups; Plant-based, Resins, and Oils.

The resins and essential oils need to be purchased for practical reasons, they only make up a relatively small, but important part of an incense mixture, and are mainly responsible for the heady and slowly evolving smell.

Plants make up the body of the incense where the mixtures of energies are released and encouraged to do their thing.

The mixture of plants used includes ones with healing abilities such as herbs.

Those with a spiritual / symbolic association such as Oak, Hawthorn or Elder.

Floral because of their cent (when fresh) and or symbolic connection.

Depending on where you live, most of these plants can easily be grown or gathered, but there may be some that will have to be purchased.

Little tip; everything will work better if you want to do it, do not make it a chore.

Whenever possible, grow, collect, dry, and prepare the plant ingredients yourself. If picked, dried, and stored properly they are generally better than shop-bought products because you know the condition of the plant when gathered, where they grew, and when and how they were collected.

An extra benefit of doing this is you always have good healthy plants for the ingredients. Growing, selecting, and collecting them yourself can also help you relax and unwind.

This also means you can harvest the parts required at the best possible time to maximise the positive outcome of their use i.e.

Season; different things are ready at different times of the year. Collect the items when they are at their best not when it is most convenient for you.

The phase of the moon; items you need that grow above ground i.e. flowers and leaves are best collected at the full moon, root items at the dark moon.

Time of day; Most things are best collected in the morning when their energy and beneficial ingredients are at their strongest, most plants tend to wilt as they warm up later in the day.

Weather conditions; The energy of some plants is not as strong in a dry spell, but the beneficial ingredients of others such as some herbs may become condensed and stronger when water is limited. Do some research and trials.

Important; Only take what you need and make sure you leave enough for the wildlife, and to grow on for next year's harvest.

Always minimise the damage to the plant and never take from a young or solitary plant, always think of the future.

A final thought; If you intend to use or create an item then do so with respect for the ingredients, be sure about the reason you are creating it, and what you want it to do.

Chapter 4

Ingredients

Plant-based parts

Item used	Reason for use
Flowers	
Clover flower	Its roots can help to bind things to the earth
Jasmin	To help calm and relax an issue
Wild Poppy	Respect for, and help from, those who have passed
Wild Rose	Female rite of passage
Trees and shrubs	
Blackthorn flower	Wild, bright, and strong, protection in future plans
Blackthorn fruit	Adds the strength and bitterness of old rituals & magic.
Elderflower	Connection with the Fae & Earth Spirits

Gorse with flower	Stop an issue returning, can strengthen moss & clover
Golden Maple leaf	Brighten past issues and future tasks
Hawthorn flower	Help the inner self heal and grow
Hawthorn berry	Strengthen the inner self
Oak leaf, young	Strengthen commitment of young males
Oak leaf, old	Male rite of passage, i.e., retirement & passing
Silver Birch bark	Encourages new life and supports life's changes
Sweet Laurel flower	Heighten and awaken the senses
Sycamore seeds	Too rise above and see the bigger picture

<u>Herbs</u>

Centaury	Calmness and knowledge of those passed
Eyebright	Focuses on the important issues

Fennel	Clean and clear any remaining obstacle
Feverfew	To see a problem calmly and without emotion
Hops	To relax and be at one with the energies
Lavender	Calms the senses and heals the body
Lemon Balm	Fresh and cleansing, penetrates an issue & area
Mint	Like Lemon Balm but gentler
Rosemary	Bind ingredients, intentions & actions together
Sage	Wisdom and experience of the issue
Valerian root	Calm and relax the inner spirit

<u>Other plant items</u>

Grass seed heads	Help problems disperse like seeds in the wind
Lynchian from a rock	Draw a problem down into the earth

Moss from a tree	Like Lynchian but gentler
Wildflower seeds	A small pinch of seeds to help future plans take root

Collecting, Drying & Storing plant material

To get the most from your chosen plant ingredients you need to take a few different factors into consideration;

Firstly; what part of the plant are you taking for use i.e., seed, flower, leaf, or root etc and what is it to be used for; thinking about these questions will help you in answering the following

1 What time of year or season will the required part be at its best?

> Blossoms, seeds & roots all have different seasons, Some leaves may be available all year round, but when will they be at their best for the intended use?

2 What phase of the moon is best to gather your items?

> Leaves & blossoms would normally be gathered at a full moon when the ingredient-rich sap is high in the plant, and roots at the dark moon when that sap has been allowed to

sink low in the plant, but it can also depend on what you are using them for.

3 Cultivated plants?

Some herbs and plants will grow happily in the house so an easy constant supply of leaves etc could always be available, but if they have been isolated from nature and the elements will the required properties within them be as strong?

4 What type and size of airtight storage vessels will you need?

Roots will normally need a larger container than seeds, blossom keeps better in a dark container, and most things are better when kept at a fairly consistent temperature and out of direct sunlight. Containers made from glass, stone or pottery are preferred for storing vessels as plastic may be affected by, or affect, the stored contents.

5 How long will the harvest take to dry and how long will it keep?

Letting items dry slowly and naturally normally allows them to retain more of the beneficial properties you want from them. How long they take to dry will depend on what you are drying, where and how you are drying them, and how long they will keep depending on their preparation and storage conditions.

Please note that you cannot use freshly gathered items they must be dried to burn properly.

There are various ways of drying the collected harvest but it needs to be done as soon as possible, do not leave the harvested material lying in a heap or bag as it will spoil.

The drying method you choose to use will partly depend on the following;

The part of the plant you are collecting i.e., seed, blossom, leaf etc

The time of year and the weather

The range of facilities you have available

The time and space required for each method

Here are some simple, commonly used methods.

Air-drying,

Stems, roots, or anything that can be tied into a small loose bundle can be hung upside down in a shady well-ventilated place, hang anything with seeds or petals over a tray or dish to catch bits that fall off. Do not make the bundles too thick or bulky as it reduces the airflow and increases the chance of them degrading and going mouldy.

Seeds, blossoms, petals etc can be laid on a sheet of paper or thin cloth (closely woven linen or cotton) over a flat wire frame to let the air circulate.

If you want to speed things up pick a warm room in the house or use the airing cupboard.

Whatever air-drying method you use keep an eye on them, and turn them around from time to time just to make sure they do not get mildew or go bad.

Forced or assisted drying,

A simple way to do this is by laying the harvested items out in a thin layer on a baking tray and putting them on very low heat in the oven. This may take minutes or hours depending on what you are drying.

Be careful, if the oven is too hot then seeds may split or "pop," blossom and petals can shrivel up beyond all recognition and some of the natural ingredients you want from it may be lost with the evaporation of the moisture within the plant.

The choice is yours, but as normal, patience and planning are required if you want the best ingredients in, and the best outcome from your incense.

Resins and essential oils

It is not practical, or possible, for most of us to gather and create our own incense resins and essential oils so these items are purchased

Incense resins.

Name Smell Suggested Use

Benzoin; Sharp & penetrating. Can make you aware of yourself & things around you

Copal, white; Uplifting & heady. Meditation & grounding

Copal, night; Thick & calming. Celebrate the darker side & focus on the light appearing.

Dragons blood; Rich, Heady & pleasing. Personal growth & commitment to new plans.

Drammer; Clean and fresh. Uplifting the spirit, good in celebration and initiation

Frankincense; Delicate, calming, feminine. Rites of passage, especially female

Myrrh; Sweet and thick, but not overpowering. Grounding, meditation. Bind troublesome spirits

Sandarose; Suttle, clean, feminine. Early female rites of passage

Sandarac; Similar to, but richer than Sandarose. Later female rites of passage.

I encourage you to burn a little of these one at a time to understand not only how the individual resins smell, but how they can affect your mood and make you feel.

Essential Oils

Name	Smell	Suggested Use

Citronella; Light, fresh lemon smell. Cleanse & clean a space or personal energies.

Clary Sage; Dull earthy smell. Wisdom, personal growth, and knowledge

Lavender; Delicate, calming, and feminine. Both calming & healing are so beneficial in most creations.

Patchouli; Pleasing, heady and floral. Calm down and lift the spirit and energies.

Petitgrain; Strong earthy citrus smell. Draw earthbound energies to clear troublesome areas.

Rose; Subtle and feminine. Mainly female rites of passage.

Scotch Pine; Strong, earthy, woodland smell. To connect with earth energies for calming and cleansing

Vanilla; Sweet and thick but not overpowering. Grounding, sombre rituals, some meditation

Those are the main items we use (Plant, Resin & Oil), but they are just a few of all the different possible ingredients available. Take the time to try each new mixture before exposing others to your creation.

See how it smells and makes you feel?

Does it fit the reason you created it?

Incense creation

This is an example of a simple incense mixture to help you understand how we use them and in what quantities, do not forget half a teaspoon of the finished mixture is all you need to cover the burn time of an average charcoal block.

This mix was created and used for clearing/cleansing an area or space.

Parts per mix	Ingredients
10	Lavender
8	Lemon Balm
2	Centaury
4	Elderflower
1	Poppy
4	Fennel
2	Gorse
2	Oak leaf, young
1	Myrrh
2	Drammer

The final choice for what essential oil to use will depend on the site and what you feel you are dealing with, but I would use a maximum of 3 or 4 drops in total of Citronella, Petitgrain or Scotch Pine.

Note; 3 – 4 drops of each are too much. Use less oil in the mixture for inside use than outside.

Do not add the oil to the mixture earlier than you need to, as it will seep into the other ingredients and change the overall smell and even the burn time.

When you put an incense mixture onto the burning charcoal the first thing you will be aware of is the smoke and smell from the oil. But the smell will start to change as the oil fades and the ground resin pieces begin to burn, it will then slowly change again as the smell of the now-burning plant items begins to mingle with the larger pieces of resin to create that final subtle mixture of smoke and smell.

With a little practice, the incense fragrance can change to suit the different stages of a ritual.

And because the average charcoal block burn time is greater than the incense, you can use one mixture to acknowledge the elements, open the area and start the ritual, and a different one to end and close.

Chapter 5

Do plants contain energy?

Plants help to create the air we breathe and are the base of our food chain, so let us look at the life force, energy, and abilities of some of the plants we share this world and our lives with.

We are not, as some people think the top of the pile, there are many other life forms that have been around a lot longer than we have, and they could live without us a lot easier than we could live without them!

What is it about open wild countryside that so appeals to many people?

Why are we fascinated by wild forests and old trees?

Why do we go to the hills and beach to unwind and relax?

Why does the Green Man image appear in so many old buildings and appeal to so many people?

Why are more and more people being drawn back to nature?

Everybody needs to find their own answers to those and other questions they may have, I can only tell you how I feel about those questions, what they mean to me, and the answers I have found.

So here are some thoughts, stories, and legends concerning trees to give you something to think about.

The following information has been put together over the years by our members and should only be used as a guide, a starting point, to help you think about and understand why a certain type of tree calls to you. It could simply be that a particular type of wood is more suitable for you to make that personal / magical tool you desire, or how its addition to an incense mix you are creating and the desired outcome could be beneficial from its addition, or it could be your personal energy needs to connect with the energy of that particular tree?

There are various books that have much more detailed information, one of which is The Celtic Wisdom of Trees by Jane Gifford, but I suggest you go out and meditate on each type of tree in turn, and maybe consider sitting with any local ones that are not listed before deciding what you do next.

When making any personal item, the material should be compatible with its creator and their reason for its creation or use, the following guide list has been compiled over the years by different people and different sources, but it works for us.

And please consider the tree when taking any wood you need.

Trees and their associations.

Alder; Masculine – a tree of the ancient Gods, its roots may decay but its wood is strong and hard-wearing when wet.

Ash; Masculine – it can be used as a link between harmony, order, truth, and justice.

Birch; Feminine - new beginnings and love. It is one of the first trees to appear in a barren area, and its short life enriches the soil for those that follow.

Blackthorn; Masculine – its thorns and fruit remind us of the bitterness of life, while its blossom shows hope for the future. Staffs made from it are associated with ancient rituals and strong magic.

Elder; Feminine –It can transport you to the realm of the fairies and is associated with transformation, regeneration, and healing.

Hawthorn; Feminine – connected to the heart and fertility. Its blossom signals the arrival of spring and begins the celebration of the new life that arrives with it.

Holly; Can be Masculine or Feminine - compassion, love, and emotions (only the female trees have berries). It is a symbol of nature's life force and it is considered most unlucky to cut one down.

Oak; Masculine – strength, protection, and honesty. Revered and respected by many cultures and is a symbol of strength and endurance. The rewards of the Oak are only given to the honest and the brave.

Rowan; Feminine - Some call it the "witch's tree"

Yew; Masculine –wisdom and protection. Its timber is said to guard the doorway between the worlds but handle it with care as all parts of the tree are poisonous.

If you want to make your own staff, late summer or early autumn is the best time of year to look for the piece of wood you need for it or any other wooden tool you are thinking of making. The trees are generally at their strongest around this time, (you do not want to make a personal tool from a diseased piece of wood) and you will do the least amount of harm to them as the flow of sap will have slowed.

If when you first find the piece you have been looking for, but find that when you connect with the tree you feel that it does not want you to take the piece from them at that time, just make a note of where it is, or leave a marker so you can find it later in the year, then return at the end of autumn or early winter and ask again.

If you go for a walk and just pick up a "piece of wood" from the floor, or cut off a random suitably looking handy branch and take it home, what you have is a stick.

It may be big enough to lean on or small enough to point with. You can whittle it, sand it down and make it look pretty, but chances are what you have created will just be a pretty stick. The chances of you forming the depth of connection that you require, or are looking for are pretty slim.

If you want a staff, wand, or any magical tool you need to put the effort into creating it, making sure it is right for you and its intended use. It is not unknown for a staff to be made from a sapling intentionally grown and shaped just for that purpose.

Trees and the wood they give us have different qualities and abilities, so before you go out with the saw and axe, do a little research, think about why you want it, what you want from it, and what you are going to do with it.

Talk to the tree in question and ask it whether you can take a piece, tell it why you want it, and listen to what it tells you.

Here is a little cautionary poem to give you something to think about.

If you cut a tree, be sure of the reason

To reduce the bleed, be sure of the season

All woods have a use, so pick the right one

All trees are different, checks should be done

They can be doorways to dreams or pathways to hell

Take your time, think hard, and make sure you pick well.

You have probably noticed a continual thread of respect for, acceptance of, and connection with, the energies of life that not only flow through Greenheart but link everything we do within it. It is this thread of respect and connection that enables us to be accepted by and at one with the wyrd and those non-tangible life forms that not only surround us, but are a part of us.

As children we are taught it is not wise to befriend strange unknown people or walk into strange or possibly dangerous situations, and neither do the non-physical / energy life forms within nature.

It seems that throughout history the majority of people who have become aware of, or come into contact with any unexplainable or non-solid life forms have classed these experiences as supernatural beings belonging to some mystical / magical realm that should be feared and destroyed.

These people and their descendants have not sought to accept and understand what those entities they encountered really were or where they fit into nature's vast tapestry of life. They simply feared what they did not understand and tried to destroy what they encountered.

Our ancestor's actions are why we are initially seen as a threat by nature's spirits and energies.

You will be accepted for your actions and thoughts, not your words.

A final thought for you on this topic, when encountering anything new we should first trust our "gut feeling" and the senses we have been given, how do these new experiences make you feel?

I suggest you welcome the unknown with caution instead of open arms until you are sure that what you are "seeing" is what is really there, and not merely what that spirit / energy wants you to see.

Just like the physical world we live in, not everything is friendly, and some life forms have their own personal agenda.

Everything we have talked about so far has looked at ways to separate the two worlds we live in. The artificial everyday world of manmade rules, possessions, ego, mistrust, and isolation. And the natural real world with its ever-turning cycle of life, the seasons that mark its turning, the life forms that rely on those seasons, and the energies that fill and power them and the life they support.

In the real world of nature, there is no pretence, or someone / something else to blame for your actions or lack of them, or a "get out of jail free card" because you only "done what it said in the book"

In the real world of nature what you get out of life depends on your attitude and what you put in.

You are now thinking how can you tell what is true or false?

How do you know what to believe?

Firstly, you need to listen to what Nature, the Energies, and that little voice in your head is saying. That little voice is not the gods speaking to and guiding you through life's troubles, it is simply your inner self drawing information from that collection of thoughts and memories within the wyrd. Use them the way you would use a personal experience to help guide you in your choices, and allow that inner knowledge to help you choose the best path to take.

Watch what is happening around you more than what you are being told.

Are those telling you how to do things walking the walk, or just talking the talk?

And most importantly trust your own feelings and intuition, trust your "gut feeling."

If what you are being told does not sound right, and / or does not feel right then smile nicely and just walk away.

I have never doubted my path, or what I have seen and experienced while walking it, but it has taken many years for me to reach this stage of acceptance and oneness. It has been interesting, surprising, and even eventful at times, and I have a feeling there is still more to come. But I have never forgotten what I was taught in those early years, to be cautious when meeting and / or investigating any new possibility before embracing the opportunity to explore, learn, and possibly make new friends.

I was taught to, and have always tried to, keep an open mind. I was also taught not to judge something or someone new, or to make up my mind too quickly and based only on first impressions, you should always try to understand something before you judge or discount it.

But I encourage you to do this from a safe distance and trust your gut.

Rituals and Celebrations

Chapter 1

When and why?

These may be held at any time, and for many different reasons, there is no right or wrong reason or time to acknowledge, give thanks for, or celebrate something, just give some thought as to why you want to do it, and its content before you start creating and doing rituals i.e. are you simply acknowledging and celebrating something, or do you need to raise energy for "magical use"?

The design, creation, personal connection and involvement required by and during these things, are, and need to be, different, each one should reflect the desire and intention that brought it into existence.

Here is a simple overview / guide of the four main reasons we hold them, just to give you something to think about;

1; Indicated by nature (as perceived by us) as a significant time of the year that should be recognised and celebrated, i.e., the seasons.

Because seasons can vary from year to year in both their starting date and their duration, their celebration dates can also not be fixed from year to year. The most suitable or significant date will be set as perceived by those holding the celebration.

These dates will by nature vary depending on where you live e.g., the May blossom will normally bloom in southern England before it does in Scotland and it may not grow at all where you live, so look at the native plants in your area and see how they fit into the season's cycle of life, watch what ones indicate the different stages.

Make a note of what shoots and buds are the first to reappear after winter.

See what native flowers appear first to bring the colour back to our surroundings.

Remember when the life around you create a new life of its own.

The harvest time along with its content and bounty will vary from place to place, along with the length and severity of winter. There is not a common date that fits these times, they always have, and always will, vary from place to place and year to year.

2; Planetary; equinoxes and solstices, these affect the seasons and are recognised for their part in turning the wheel of life.

They have an almost fixed date from year to year so are easier to plan for and arrange.

3; Lunar; the four phases of the moon, Dark, Waxing, Full, and Waning.

These affect every living thing on this planet from the germination of seeds to the height of the ocean's tides, and are respected and celebrated for their strength and beneficial powers.

The moon has an approximate 28-day cycle, so these also have a known plannable date that may coincide with, and be incorporated into a seasonal celebration if wanted or needed.

4; Personal; these may be;

A rite of passage i.e. a birth, handfasting, croneing or death.

A ritual created to resolve a personal problem, or to mark and acknowledge an achievement or milestone in your life.

Or to simply celebrate your life, abilities, and gifts.

Whatever the chosen reason for creating and doing one, all rituals are held in an atmosphere of communal oneness, recognition, and thanks.

Avoid the temptation to create a ritual or celebration for something simply because you enjoy doing it. When your focus and goal is the "warm fuzzy feeling" you get after doing one, then you are doing them for the wrong reason, you are losing that connection with nature, and the possible benefit from that connection, these events will simply exist to massage your ego.

Wheel of the Year celebrations.

In today's world it seems to be common for people to acknowledge and celebrate a date printed in a diary because they believe that must be the correct and only time to hold a ritual for the purpose of celebrating a particular event. Sadly, many of those dates seem to have been selected without consulting those who have been acknowledging these events for a very long time.

Why? Possibly to give regulation to modern life and separate it from nature's natural cycles?

Nature and its cycles of life do not work to a calendar with set dates and neither do the seasons.

For example; the Hawthorn normally blooms earlier in Cornwall than it does in Scotland so why should we all celebrate May Day on the 1st of May?

The 1st of May only became a May Day Bank Holiday in 1976.

Mayday should be celebrated when the May blossom is present on a chosen tree in the area where you live. If there are no Hawthorn bushes in your area then a suitable alternative is chosen by the local group / coven that will make you aware of this special time approaching.

In Greenheart we do not just have a series of "special" dates written in our diaries along with details of what to do on those dates. We have times throughout the year that we know are part of the cycles of life, they have meaning to nature, and to us, and they are acknowledged and celebrated with purpose and respect.

This is a brief overview of the Greenheart annual celebrations. Note the connections between them, and how one relies on and supports another.

Our intention is to reflect on, acknowledge, and work with nature's seasonal connections.

The times / dates for the seasonal ones may seem a little vague, but they are held to coincide with a natural event that can vary from year to year, and place to place.

The main stages of nature we acknowledge and celebrate in (UK East Anglia) Greenheart are;

Returning life: When life starts to awake from winter's rest. Early February

The time of "Returning life" is celebrated when new growth becomes visible once again in the dormant soil and at the tips of seemingly lifeless plants.

(A different type of plant may be used in different areas as very little grows anywhere and everywhere, try to use the natural local plants and not an imported one)

Having made it through the cold barren time of winter, the re-appearance of life brings hope for the future, it is celebrated with a ritual to acknowledge the passing of those hard, cold, days, and the promise of what is to come. It will include the scattering of grain and seeds kept from the previous year as acknowledgement and thanks, some to grow and some to share with the life around us.

The scattered items are selected and kept from the last harvest celebration for this purpose.

The feast is a simple one, using ingredients from the last harvest to celebrate and encourage the one to come.

Spring Equinox; March 20th?

The time of balance between dark and light. The point when light and life once more regain the upper hand in the circle of life.

The days are getting longer and warmer with the promise of good times ahead. A good time to connect with nature and the energies of life.

A time to revisit and confirm your plans for the coming year. (The plans you made at the winter solstice.)

The improving weather is acknowledged and celebrated with a fire to support, encourage, and strengthen the new sun.

The feast is simple but bright and made from a mix of stored and fresh items.

New life: When the May blossom opens and new life starts to surround us

A time to celebrate the creation of new life, various birds and animals are rearing a new generation and everything is acknowledging the pleasures, sensations, gifts, and abilities that are a part of life.

Garlands and posies of blossom and spring flowers are created for, or during this spring celebration, with some being kept for use in the second harvest celebration later in the year.

Some of the new growth from the seeds scattered in February should also be acknowledged and used if possible.

The feast consists mainly of fresh produce and pastries that awake and please the senses, with the new year's produce clearly visible amongst the food and drink.

Midsummer; Summer Solstice June 21st?

A time of rest, peace, and pleasure.

A time to acknowledge, and enjoy, the long summer days and their warm sensual nights.

The crops are grown, and the harvest they carry is maturing and ripening.

A time to be proud of, and reflect upon the hard work involved in helping this happen.

And a time to acknowledge the sacrifice these crops will make for our future.

The Yule log is selected at this time and then prepared and kept for the Yule fire.

The feast shall reflect the rich and varied bounty available to us at this time.

This is a good time to talk about our hopes and desires for the future, these are not firm oaths and promises, but hopes and dreams.

First Harvest: Grain; July / August depending on crops and weather

A time to give thanks for the harvest that will, if used wisely, see us through the harder times ahead.

Corn dollies, twists and other items are made / used during the celebration, and some are then kept along with grains and fruit for the Yule and Returning life celebrations.

This time of bountiful food should mark and celebrate not just the harvest gifts, but also the busy time and hard work for those bringing in the harvest and storing it for future needs.

The feast shall be rich and plentiful, but not wasteful, and shared with the life around us.

Autumn Equinox; September 23rd?

A time of balance between dark and light, when the cold damp hand of death once more gains the upper hand in its constant battle with life.

The green wood knows it will soon be time for it to withdraw into the earth to prepare for the year to come, and once more the dark wood will become home and larder to wildlife in the cold dark times ahead.

The feast shall reflect the sacrifice the green wood has made, and the dark wood will make in caring for the life that will depend on them.

It should be bright, warming and contain the seasonal foods that will not keep through the cold times ahead.

Second Harvest; Autumn/start of winter October/November when the leaves are falling and life begins to prepare for winter

Also known as the Blood harvest because in times past you would know how much feed you had to see you and the animals through winter, and any live-stock you could not feed though-out the winter season would be killed and eaten or preserved.

The long cold nights ahead see physical growth overshadowed by internal reflection.

This is a time to reflect on our actions during the past year, and understand and learn from their outcome, also a time to consider our plans for the future.

A time to remember and acknowledge, those that have helped us on our journey through life, and those who no longer stand beside us.

The garlands, posies and sprigs from the spring celebration are burnt along with the things you do not want to take into the future (negative actions and thoughts etc).

The ritual should have a calm, relaxed atmosphere.

It is too late to worry about being prepared for winter, the preparation and work should have been carried out in the growing season, and it is now too late to lament what you should have done then.

The feast is simple but substantial, reflecting its blood harvest name. It is warm hearty food that will help to prepare us for the hard times ahead.

Winter Solstice: December 21st?

The nights are long and becoming colder, life has prepared physically for this time we call winter, now we should prepare mentally for the year ahead.

This is the time to acknowledge the short days, dying sun and everything you have because of them.

But it is also the time to celebrate the new growing sun and the long warm days it will bring.

The Yule log that was chosen at the summer solstice, and the straw creations from the harvest celebration, are burnt while plans for the coming year are discussed and agreed upon during the feast.

The cold, still, time of winter should be used to think about and prepare plans for the coming year.

This is the time to talk about and confirm our plans for the coming year with oaths and promises.

The feast should be substantial and warming and leave you with a contented feeling.

Chapter 2

Ritual content

The contents of a ritual or celebration will depend on the reason for its creation, but no two rituals will, or should be, exactly the same. Even regular annual events such as an equinox or harvest celebration will vary from year to year, because we and the world around us change from year to year, and a ritual should reflect those that are taking part as well as the reason for it being held, and the contents of the feast afterwards.

Greenheart rituals are generally simple events; Incense is used to mark the beginning and to help awaken everyone's senses, candles are lit as focal points for the Old Ones and Elements as each is being acknowledged and welcomed.

Other tools or personal items may be added and used at times, but that will depend on why the ritual is being held, the sequence of actions within it, and the words used during it.

Working outside in nature is preferred, but we accept that being outside is not always possible or practical.

Generally, a celebration or ritual is pre-written and planned, with a practice run held beforehand so all involved know what is expected of them, important parts are sometimes read from notes during the proceedings, but this does not mean everything has to be memorised and word perfect, so long as all involved know what they are doing, where they should be, what they have to say, and most important of all, why they are doing it, everything should all go smoothly. People bumping into each other because they do not know what happens next, tends to have a negative effect on the group's ability to reach a successful Altered State of Consciousness which is required to attain the desired connection with the elemental energies.

The required level of an ASC and connection will vary with the type of ritual being held. A seasonal celebration can be a light hearted get together, designed, and created to give thanks for the harvest etc.

A rite of passage created to celebrate someone's life and passing should be a meaningful event to celebrate their achievements, or to mark and acknowledge their energy returning to the wyrd while ensuring their memory lives on.

A few important things to adhere to at a ritual, and most other times are;

When the celebration / ritual is complete we do not say farewell to the Elements as they do not leave us.

This is for practical reasons; The elements do not, and cannot leave us, as we, and everything else is created from, and by them, where would they go?

On a simpler note, do you really want air and the other elements to leave you? They maintain our ability to breathe and live.

If you leave an offering ensure it is something that is of use to other life forms Water, grains, and fruit are preferred, alcohol, sticky or shiny thing at best have no practical use in nature, and can also harm the smaller things.

When working outside leave only footprints, and take only memories.

This is not "our world" we must be considerate to those we share it with, and those we will eventually leave it to.

If it is of no use to the life in the place you use, and cannot be re-absorbed into the earth without damaging the life that relies on that earth, then take it away with you.

Chapter 3

Preparation and method

I thought this would be a good time to remind you that there are no Gods and Goddesses in Greenheart, apart from us.

We have nothing to worship, upset or blame.

We take full responsibility for our lives and our actions.

We play the game with the cards we are delt, we know and accept it is not possible to ask for another go because we did not like the outcome.

All things are part of the "one thing" which we refer to as the **Old Ones.** These are not human in form or character. They are energy, the beginning and end of everything, they are the origin and sustainer of life.

"They" will not do your bidding, and cannot be "offended," never forget that we are just another little insignificant part in that circle of life.

The five elements do not have form or feelings and cannot be upset or offended, they are aspects of the Old Ones. They are different ingredients from the same thing that when mixed in the correct proportions can create wondrous things such as planets and the life upon them.

This is how we think of the Old Ones and Elements.

The Old-ones; The origin, sustainer, and the end of everything!

Pure Energy, it exists in the things that are, and the things that are not.

Earth; The bread of life. This is the physical beginning and end of all life.

Whether it is Animal, Mineral or Vegetable, the planet that sustains us, or the universe we live in, if it is matter then it is Earth, and Earth supplies the "food" for physical life as we know it.

Water; The blood of life, this flows through the rivers and seas of the planets, the veins of trees, animals, and us. It travels around the earth's surface and through its skies, it can be powerful or soothing and is essential for the continued existence of all life as we know it on this planet.

Air; The breath of life, like water is not bound to the earth and can travel at will.

It can be a gentle soothing breeze or an uncontrollable force, but again, it is essential for life as we know it.

The part we humans need most may be a waste product of other life, but that is how the wheel turns.

Fire; The light of life.

Throughout the universe there are planets like the sun, these burning giants of fire light the skies and warm other planets such as the earth, and the life upon them.

Ether; Ether, the spark of life. Ether is different from the other elements in that it is a non-tangible thing / substance / entity, call it what you will.

It is that spark of life that enters a seed when it germinates and encourages it to grow.

When the other Elements combine to create a pool of mud, it is Ether that adds that spark to some unseen molecule that gives it the opportunity to grow and develop.

It does not "give life," but it gives the possibility for life to happen.

We work in a circle (as shown below) moving clockwise, in the same direction as the sun and moon.

Incense is placed on the burning block then the old ones at the centre are acknowledged before we welcome the elemental energies, one at a time, in the order shown;

1, Earth. **2,** Water. **3,** Air. **4,** Fire, and **5,** Ether, then returning to Earth to complete the energy connections that are around, and within, the area we are working in.

We normally do this by lighting a candle for each one in turn, while saying a few words to acknowledge and welcome them as you would an old trusted friend, their presence is affirmed and felt by all present as the candle flame grows and steadies before moving to the next one.

The shape you see below is not thought of or used as a Pentagram or mark of the Devil.

Leonardo DaVinci did not draw a pentagram, and NASA did not put the Sign of the Devil on their space probes. They simply happen to look very similar to a commonly used new age symbol.

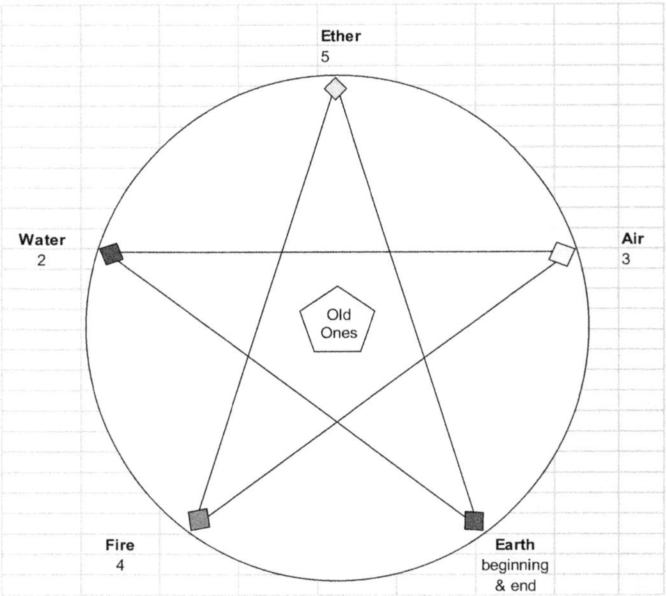

Entrance & Exit

The circle is laid out and opened in this manner for two reasons.

Laid out this way; with Energy (Old Ones) at its centre supporting the five Elements, who create and support the outer circle (Circle of Life)

Opened this way; when you prepare ground for planting you start with the earth, then you add the water, next you ensure an air supply, then you warm it, before finally planting the seed and smoothing the earth.

Who are we to disagree with Nature?

It also mirrors the human form;

Legs; Earth and Fire

Arms; Air and Water

Head; Ether

Heart and lungs; The Old Ones (Source of energy)

Outer body shell; our aura and senses that connect with the energies of life

This is not created as a "magical" or "protective" place, a circle is simply the easiest shape to lay out and work in.

We do not need, or want a shield of any kind, our desire and intention is to contact and be as one with the elements and energies, this is not possible with fear or doubt in your heart and mind.

Any, and all "power" required is built up by, and then released from, those within the circle area.

Circle location, orientation, and size;

Its location will depend on available space and locations in your area. Ideally, it needs to be somewhere outside with nature where you will not be disturbed while working in this special place you have created.

Its orientation needs to "feel" right when you walk into it, we suggest you have the entrance in the South which places Ether in the North. But this is not set in stone, create and use what "feels right" for the place you are in.

Its size. There needs to be enough room to move freely without bumping into things or other people, 12 to 15 feet across is generally large enough but this will depend on the number of people.

The centre table or Alter has a **Y-shaped** piece of wood on it to represent the male and female, both of them are needed and work with Ether in the creation of life. A life rooted in the Old One's ever-flowing energy.

Male Female

Y

Old Ones

When preparing and opening the circle the candle / incense for the Old Ones is placed at the bottom leg of the **Y** and any other items required for the ritual are placed around it.

Different areas inside the circle seem to be naturally in tune with different parts and requirements of life.

Strength, Courage, and Protection are at the entrance to the circle between Earth and Fire which are both strong physical Elements.

Compassion, Feelings, and Empathy are on the left with Fire and Water, both of these are able to excite and destroy, and both are needed by Ether to create.

Knowledge, Wisdom, and Patiance on the right, with Earth holding the Knowledge of all that has gone before, Air carrying their memories and Wisdom, and Patiance is required for both. These are also needed by Ether to create new life.

None of these are waiting patiently for you to contact them and ask for their help.

Think of them as being an exclusive club with very good member benefits, but a very strict set of rules, and they are not going to change those rules just to suit you.

These rules are not written down for you, they are in the life and seasons all around you.

You must take the time to watch and understand how nature works, and you must be prepared to understand, accept, and be a part of it.

Always remember that you want to be accepted by **Nature's Elemental Energies,** and possibly benefit from that acceptance. **Nature** wants and will gain nothing from your presence.

Chapter 4

Preparing and Opening the Circle

Even though each celebration and ritual may be different from the last, or the next, the way we open the circle to welcome and acknowledge the elements and energies before connecting with them remains the same. We do this for our benefit not for theirs. We normally use the same words and actions to acknowledge and welcome the Elements when opening the circle as this helps us create a natural rhythm that allows everyone to know what is happening without having to think about it, which in turn allows everyone to relax, which is essential to obtain an ASC which is needed for the connection and oneness that is desired and required.

An individual's frame of mind, attitude and demeanour, the way you feel and act while laying out the circle and lighting the candles can affect the desired outcome, even how you feel while making the incense is important.

When the circle is prepared with everything required in the right place, the incense block is lit, then all leave the circle area and take a few moments to prepare themselves ready to begin the ritual.

When all are ready, we walk through the entrance in the correct order and clockwise around the alter, so when we stop nobody needs to move to let someone else by because they are in the wrong place.

A smooth, uneventful sequence of events helps create a positive outcome to the planned event.

We then stand in silence for a few seconds to centre ourselves before the ritual begins.

All turn to face each candle as it is lit and the words are spoken, then stand in silent thought while the flame steadies as each (Old Ones and Elements) are felt to enter the circle area with us.

The person acting as Alter is simply the person chosen to, or who feels they need to, play this part in the proceedings.

There is no leader or person in charge, we all do what we are good at, and learn from those who know more than ourselves.

Please note that the words I have used in the rituals are not set in stone and can be changed if they do not "feel right" or fit the reason for their use. But give any new words some thought, and try to make them" flow" with a rhythm and continuation that fits the actions, meaning, and desired outcome of the ritual.

The chosen person stands at the bottom of the Altar and places incense on the burning block.

Then lights the candle for the Old Ones and says;

The Old Ones
You were at the beginning
You sustain all life
You shall be at the end
Come join our circle
Let us be as one

All say; **Let us be as one.**

They move to the Earth position light the candle and say;

Earth
The bread of life
You put flesh on our bones
You give us form
Come join our circle
Let us be as one

All say; **Let us be as one.**

They move to the water position light the candle and say;

Water
The Blood of Life
You fill our veins
You give us strength
Come join our circle
Let us be as one

All say; **Let us be as one.**

They move to the Air position light the candle and say;

Air
The breath of life
You fill our lungs
You awake our senses
Come join our circle
Let us be as one

All say; **Let us be as one.**

They move to the Fire position light the candle and say;

Fire
The light of life
You warm our blood
You fuel our passions
Come join our circle
Let us be as one

All say; **Let us be as one.**

They move to the Ether position light the candle and say;

Ether
The cauldron of life
The spark of creation
You make life possible
Come join our circle
Let us be as one

All say; **Let us be as one.**

Now read those words again, think about what those words are saying, think about the meaning behind them and how it fits the creation and continuation of life.

Meditate on each one, how does it make you feel?

The spoken words should awaken and call to the energies within you, you are not speaking to an external otherworldly being, but to that part of "It" that exists within you. These words should help connect you with the Elemental Wyrd, and everything that flows within it.

I suggest you use these words, these statements of how you feel for this purpose until they become part of a smooth transition and connection with the Energies and Elements that dwell within yourself. Always remember that you are not talking to an omnipotent being who looks after you, but the spark of creation that dwells within you, and the energies that created and maintain the amazing living being that is you.

Once you are able to walk into the circle and feel their presence without words or actions you may be tempted to skip what some may see as an unnecessary part of the ritual, but this would be like not opening a door because you know what is on the other side, instead of just leaving out acknowledging the old ones and energies, you could simplify it by speaking to them as a group while slowly walking around the circle with something like;

Elements and energies of this place
We ask you to acknowledge and join with us.

At this time of celebration?
or
To be part of our ritual?

Come join our circle.
Let us be as one

All say; **Let us be as one.**

I urge you to make that personal connection something that happens automatically before you start leaving stages out of what is a progressive event containing different stages.

A little step not taken now could cause you to stumble further along your path.

That is an example of how the circle area can be prepared and energised ready for those within to begin their ritual.

When the ritual is complete, the altar closes the circle by adding more incense to the block and saying the following before leading everyone to the feast.

We are created from and remain part of
The elements and energies of life
We do not say farewell,
For we do not part,

We now ask you to join us in the feast.

The candles and incense are left to burn as all calmly leave the circle for the feast.

The "feast" has two purposes, firstly it completes the evening by allowing all present to relax and talk with friends and colleagues.

And secondly, it helps with what is known as "grounding" the act of reconnecting the physical and spiritual parts of you so they work as one, and having something to eat and drink helps to awaken the physical you as the act of eating, swallowing, and digestion involves many different areas of the body, and doing this can help all those who took part to reconnect their physical and spiritual sides which may be necessary (if they are driving) for them arrive home safely.

<u>Important.</u>

When working outside, leave only footprints, and take only memories.

This is not only "our world", we must be aware of those we share it with, and those who will follow us.

So, when all is finished and complete, the items (including any rubbish) are packed away and removed.

Ensure any offering is of use to the other life forms that share the space. Fruit's, grains, and water are the most welcome and safest offerings to leave, anything sticky, processed or alcoholic may harm or even kill the native life in that space / area.

Please be aware there are those who may have their own personal agenda and reason for doing things that others may not be aware of, and if all present are not of the same mind, if one person has their own agenda or reason for being there i.e. they just want to be part of a group / coven so they can tell their friends and acquaintances, are not as committed or true in their belief, or have this desire to create and be part of a hierarchy within a group, they can stop you obtaining the desired effect from a ritual, cause friction and discontent between the members, and may eventually cause the groups breakup.

Chapter 5

Ritual content

We have looked at how we acknowledge, welcome, and become one with the elements and energies while opening the circle area in preparation for a ritual, so now we will look at what a ritual may contain and consist of.

A rituals creation and content will vary depending on the season it is held, and the reason for its creation and use, as will the items required on the alter during that ritual.

To open and prepare the area / circle for a ritual you will normally need, 6 candles (and something to light them with), that is 1 on the alter to welcome the Old Ones and 5 around the circle's edge to welcome the elements, plus an incense burner with charcoal block and incense to “set the mood and help open the door” so to speak.

For the actual ritual, you may need a goblet and drink, a small dish with anointing oil, an offering dish, other candles, another incense burner with charcoal block and incense, or personal items of some kind. Or none of the above, there are no must-have items, and no right or wrong way, all I will say is that when you begin holding celebrations and rituals, a few special symbolic items can help things become more active and strengthen the overall feeling, connection, and outcome.

So, for now, I will just say the altar would be set out, and contain, all that is needed for, and during the ritual.

This is an example of a Winter Solstice (the shortest day) celebration ritual. It has been created not only to mark and acknowledge a specific time in the ever-changing seasons in the wheel of life, but to also reflect how we feel about that time and its implications.

Again, the words would be spoken by Alter (a chosen person) who would begin by saying;

We gather here to celebrate the Winter Solstice and its place in the ever-turning circle of life.

The dark cold nights of winter are a time of death and decay.

A time to shelter and rest

And yet this darkness is also a time of rebirth for the sun.

A time to acknowledge the new life it will bring, along with the hopes and promises for the coming year.

Alter then puts more incense on the burning block, and all take a few seconds to think about what this means to them. Alter then says

We acknowledge, and are thank-full for the harvest sacrifices that allow us to pass safely through the cold long nights ahead, and into the new growing sun.

May the flames from the celebration fire give power to the growing sun and the New Year it will bring.

They raise the goblet high and say;

To the returning sun

All say;

To the returning sun

Alter sips from the goblet then it is passed around the group (In today's world of fear some may prefer there-own cup). As each person takes it, they say a few words from their heart before they raise it in acknowledgement, take a sip, and pass it on until it returns to the altar.

May the energy we draw on and use in these long winter nights be returned by the new life, and our actions, in the coming year

All say;

So will it be

The candles are left to burn out as all leave the circle for the feast where the Yule log is placed on the fire, then the straw creations from the Harvest ritual are placed in the flames with words of thanks for the harvest bounty before the feast begins and plans for the coming year are made.

If you are just starting on this path then you will not have a Yule log or straw creations from the last harvest, so just mention the items, confirm your beliefs and reason for holding this ritual, and prepare for next year.

The intention, focus and desire within Greenheart is to be at one with nature (that is all of nature, animal, vegetable, mineral and cosmic) and to know and accept our place in the circle of life.

Doing this allows us to develop that connection with the elements and energies, which in-turn allows us to connect with, and draw upon the knowledge and experience of those that went before, and those who share, use, and depend upon those energies today.

Personal Dedication & Commitment Ritual

Chapter 1

Confirming your beliefs.

I have tried to explain to you the simple basics of what we do, tell you why we do it, and what it means to us, and I have tried to give you an idea of what it can enable you to do. But to really be accepted by, and at one with nature and the elemental energies, to connect with the wyrd and its memories and knowledge, you must be true in your thoughts and actions, you must be committed and constant in your beliefs. On the plus side, doing this can also strengthen your personal protective aura.

A lot of people pay simple lip service to their beliefs and methods of acknowledging those beliefs. Some say they follow a "Pagan" path without really understanding what that word originally meant and why they are doing the things asked of them. And some will follow the most popular, or easiest path just to be part of the current trend.

I encourage you to look into the original meaning of a word before using it to describe yourself.

Explore the origin of the actions and events you are being expected to take part in.

Think about and look into what some of the items currently in use were originally created for before you place them onto your altar, or include them in a ritual.

Take time to think about, and explore what you believe, why you believe it, and if it is truly right for you. Once you are certain that your path is the right one for you, and the tools and actions used within that belief reflect how you feel about life, nature, and all that it encompasses you may want to confirm those beliefs, and your commitment to that belief with a rite of passage to mark this important step in your journey, so I have added a little ritual that may help you with this, once again the words are not set in stone and should be adjusted as seen fit by the person taking that next step, we shall call them the "Initiate."

Chapter 2

Taking that first step.

Preparing the circle;

Prepare the Alter and circle as described and shown earlier, plus 1 extra charcoal block with its holder, 1 extra candle with its holder (a symbol of the next stage you are entering in your journey), extra drink to refill the goblet and fruit & grain to share with the life around them.

Other personal items may be added if you feel they are needed.

Opening the circle;

The circle is opened as normal by alter who then says why we are here;

We gather here to acknowledge __ *the initiates name here* **_ _ finding their path, and now wish to confirm their intentions and commitment to that path.**

The Initiate steps forward and adds incense to their charcoal block then silently considers what they are about to do, and what it will mean to them now and for the future. They then confirm their intensions by raising their head to the stars and saying:

Ones of Old

Energies of life

I come here to confirm my commitment to my beliefs

And to the Energies, I am a part of

They circle the alter stopping at the top, and light their new candle from the Old One's candle before raising their head and saying;

I am part of life's creations.

I glory in my gifts and abilities.

I revel in my sensual pleasures.

I rejoice in having found my way to this path.

I will try to tread a path that is true, on this journey with no end.

This is my pledge

And thus, will it be.

They raise the goblet to the old ones before taking a sip and placing it back on the alter and circling it 3 times while chanting.

I am you

You are me

We are one

And shall always be

When finished all stand in silent contemplation before the initiate refills the goblet and passes it around the circle while saying

As we share this drink, so we share this life.

With it, I affirm my commitment to this path.

And my conviction to enjoy the gifts and abilities I possess

To live my life to the full

And to pass on what I have learnt

This is my oath

They stand silent for a moment to contemplate their words.

Alter then steps forward and says;

They have stated their commitment in words.

Now let them draw on your strength to turn those words into actions.

You have joined us in this ritual, now join us in our feast.

Another pinch of incense is placed on the incense blocks and their ritual is complete.

Closing the circle;

The circle is closed and all leave the area as described earlier.

The feast should reflect the importance of the special event that has just taken place.

A word of caution

Do not do this ritual unless you mean it?

Your words and actions will be noted and remembered

They will be remembered by those who share this personal moment in time with you, and it will be noted by your ancestors who control that little voice in the back of your head.

Do I need to explain about the chant?

I suppose I should explain the reason and thought behind the words.

This is being said to the elements and energies within us, not to any external deity but the elements and energies we came from, are still a part of, and will return to.

I am you

We came from and are made of the Elemental Energies of life.

You are me

Those Energies continue to maintain that which we are made of.

We are one

Nature's Elemental Energies are our origin, existence, and destination.

And shall always be.

This is how it has always been, and shall always be.

The grammar may not be the best, but the feelings and intentions within it should come from the heart, Greenheart.

It is normally said three times, starting quite low and calm then getting stronger and more positive with each round, but never a shout.

Sometimes you may feel like dancing around the circle while saying it, that just happens rather than being planned. If it doesn't disrupt the planned event, go with your feelings.

This chant can be used internally to help focus during a meditation.

To confirm your feelings in a personal event like a rite of passage.

Or to build focus and connection when drawing on and building energy for use in a "magical" ritual, it all depends on your frame of mind, why it is being used, and the way it is said.

I suggest you take time to think about and meditate on how the chant makes you feel and what you would use it for before actually using it.

I said at the beginning this is not an easy, quick fix path, and as with anything worthwhile to get the most out of something, you must be prepared to put in the work.

Think about things before you just give it a try to see how it goes.

Have you considered and are you prepared for what could happen, as opposed to what you would like to happen?

Spend some time practising aspects until they feel comfortable, natural, and the right thing to do for the purpose they are being used.

If you are prepared to put in the time and effort, then I am sure your abilities will develop along with your knowledge.

This Belief, Knowing, Way of life, call it what you will that is Greenheart can be a doorway to so many other nature-based things, and generally, as your connection with nature becomes stronger and easier to achieve, so will your empathic connection to life around you, so do not be surprised if you unexpectedly find yourself feeling happy, sad, or wanting to cry for some unknown reason.

As your connection with the energies develops so will your inner strength, leaving you calmer and stronger.

The world we are forced to be a part of will seem to hold fewer fears and dangers (nature is no longer allowed to cure the stupidity of man so we learn to tolerate it)

Let Us Go a Little Deeper

Chapter 1

Where do we go from here?

How can we pull everything we have looked at so far together and make it work as one?

Your personal outlook, attitude, and commitment are the main things that will control, and limit your progress and development, and you need to have an open mind when confronted with something new, do not believe or discount something new based on other people's opinions or comments, or your current knowledge and experiences, just accept the possibility of new possibilities, and take it from there.

Here is a little level two guided meditation on water, where visualization can not only help you "see" things but also "feel" and "experience" them. This one was created to help understand and experience the element of water, it may take a few sessions before you fully experience the power and essence of water, but it should come with time and practice.

A guided meditation to explore water.

Sit comfortably, if possible, place your feet flat on the floor but not too close together, have your hands and arms supported and resting comfortably, now wriggle about a little to get settled down in your seat, with your back supported, head balanced and your mind and body relaxed, and at ease.

Now take a few slow, deep, breaths, with each breath feel your lungs slowly fill, and then empty again, feel the air flow in and fill every tiny part of your being, then leave you more relaxed as you breathe out.

Feel your heart beating gently inside you, listen to its calm, soothing, beat.

Feel how it beats out that constant, smooth rhythm of life.

As you take your next breath you become aware of sensations in your feet, they seem to be spreading, merging with the ground, you feel a calm tingling sensation flowing up from the earth, through your feet, into your calf's, and beyond.

You feel that tingle in your thighs, it's warm and relaxing, each time you breathe in you feel it being pulled up through your legs, filling the pit of your stomach, the very centre of your being.

It travels higher with every breath, expanding your senses, making it hard to tell where you stop and the universe begins.

Each time you breathe out you can feel yourself relax that little bit more as the tension and problems of life just fade away.

With your next breath that tingle fills your chest, and overflows down into your arms, swelling your hands, pushing the senses in your fingers to their limit, allowing you to touch, and feel the air around you.

You now feel it travel up into your neck and shoulders, just roll your head a little to release any last traces of tension, then as you breathe out let that tension float up and out of your body, leaving you calm and relaxed.

Now in your own time, leaving your physical self behind, stand up and walk towards the open door in front of you, when you are ready, step through the door and into a small garden.

It is early morning and the dew glistens in the sunlight like pearls on a brightly coloured gown, a path through these glistening jewels leads down to a gate gently swinging between two willow trees, and as you walk along you can feel the early morning mist rising into the sunlight.

Reaching the open gate, you look out onto a meadow of grass that moves in the breeze like ripples on a pond, just stand and gaze at this sea of living colour before walking between the willows, through the gate, and out into that meadow.

Entering the meadow, you see there are many well-trodden paths branching out in different directions, each with its own destination.

We are going to follow the path on the left that leads down into a sandy patch of scrubland, so we turn and start our journey through a sea of swaying grass.

As you walk along you notice that the types of plant and soil are slowly changing, the grass has become coarser, the shrubs stunted and more robust, and the soil beneath your feet has become sandy. Looking up you see that you have walked onto a beach with the waves gently lapping the shore.

The rhythmic sound of the waves on the beach, and the sea spray in the air makes your skin tingle, but you feel safe on this deserted shore, you know that somebody, or something is watching over you.

As you slowly walk towards the water, ever closer to those gently lapping waves, your bare feet reach that point where land and sea combine, one merging into the other.

And as the water gently washes over your skin, you feel a sense of wellbeing, something is calling you into the water, into that clear, blue, ocean.

You enter the clear blue sea willingly, almost excitedly, and as you do so energy and power seem to enter and coarse through your body.

Once in the water you find that not only can you breathe normally, but your movements are so fluid, and so natural that you can swim better than the fish around you.

You feel at one with the water and head out excitedly into the open sea, revelling in the freedom of movement and space.

You dive deep into the murky depths where there is no light or sound, then turn and head back to the surface light with a speed and power that you did not think possible until reaching the surface with such power that waves are sent crashing up the beach, only to roll slowly back towards you.

As these waves roll back to you, you realise that the fish that swim within them are also swimming within you, through you. You have become their world, their source of life.

As you watch, and feel, these life forms moving about freely in their world, you and the sea become calm. And as you do so, you relax and float gently to the surface where the next wave carries you smoothly to the shore, laying you softly on the beach.

The spent waves return gently to the sea, and you find that once again, you are on dry land looking out over the ocean. Your cloths show no signs of your journey, only the footsteps in the sand reassure you that it was not a dream.

But now it is time to leave this world of water, so taking one last look around you turn and walk across the beach, back through the rough grasses and sandy scrub towards the meadow. The breeze has died away now and the grass stands still and motionless as you walk along beside it.

The willow trees are just up ahead with the gate standing open between them. Another few steps and you are back at the gate, you take one last look around you before stepping through the gate, and back into the garden, where once again you follow the short path up to the house, step through the doorway, and back inside.

Walking over to your resting body, you sit down and rejoin your physical self.

Now in your own time, open your eyes, take a deep breath, and return to the here and now.

How did you feel while doing that meditation?

Could you feel the power of the water and its waves?

Did you become a part of the journey and experience, or were you watching from the shoreline?

At first, you may only be aware of a sound or feeling, you may "know" where you are, but do not feel a part of what is around you. Time, practice, and patience should pull the picture together for you. I could sense and feel things a long time before I could see them, and sometimes the information just pops into my head like a memory, but however it comes to you trust and believe in yourself and your abilities.

When opening the circle for a ritual or celebration I can see and feel the Old Ones and Elements appear and join us. I can feel the energy build and grow as each one is welcomed, and I can feel the area within the circle become warm as it gains a positive charge.

Even though this was, and still is a mainly oral path we have always been encouraged to record the areas we were given to think about, explore and experience, to make notes for future reference and comparison, and to help explain to others how we arrived at this place in time with the abilities and knowledge we now possess. This is something I wrote after being asked how I learnt to do what I do, and what I know, how did I find out about these abilities, and where did I look for the information?

We had all been talking about our personal journeys in our search for "The Craft" so that is what I called it.

MY SEARCH FOR THE CRAFT. September.2003.

My search has been a journey of discovery that has spanned the greater part of my life, and I am sure will carry on for the remaining time I have left.

This journey has taken me along many paths, some have been dead ends so to speak where you could spend an eternity studying something, trying to find that magical spark, that holy grail, and never get any closer to your desired quests end than when you first began your journey.

I have walked along winding paths that twist and turn leaving you unsure of where you are, or what you are looking for, only to find yourself back where you started, no wiser, just a little more confused.

At first, I thought I knew what I was looking for and where to look. It took quite a while for me to realise that I had been looking in the wrong place. That does not mean that I suddenly knew where the right place was, that took a bit longer to discover and the first thing I realised after looking in the right place was that I did not know what I was looking for, or to put it another way, everything I thought I knew up to that point basically proved how little I knew!

So, after many years seeking that "truth" that answer to the unanswerable question, I had found a starting point, a place to begin my search in earnest.

The next few years past and I realised that the truth does not exist, and if the question is unanswerable then I am wasting my time trying to answer it.

I was finally getting somewhere, but I still did not know where it was that I was getting to, or even if I wanted to go there.

As time passed a mental picture of my quest started to form. OK it was as clear as a thick fog on a dark night, but the outline was taking shape, and even though I still did not have answers to most of my questions, at least I had stopped beating myself up trying to answer them, so things were improving.

That brings things up to date really. There have been a few more steps forward so to speak. The vision of my quest has become slightly clearer these past years, I do not know how many answers to the original questions I have found, or if it is just that I have stopped looking for answers that were not really needed.

The pace of my search feels calmer these days, it seems less intense yet more productive, but that could be because some of the things I was searching for in the past, now travel with me on my journey.

That was over twenty-five years ago, and since then I have learnt not to look for things, but to explore possibilities, accept what I find or am given, and take it from there.

Over the years I have discovered how to be at one with the residual energies of life that has gone before, memories of events that are held within the earth, and contact life forms I was not previously aware of. I also accept that I still know so little, and there is still so much more to learn.

Meditation and visualization are very useful tools when exploring new possibilities, but having someone who accepts and shares your beliefs and desires, someone you can trust, someone to explore and learn with will be a great benefit for both of you.

Ideally you will find someone who can help and guide you along your chosen path, but to find and become part of a working group would give you the chance of learning through practical experience in a safe guided environment, where you could be involved in and learn new things with an experienced person watching over you.

Chapter 2

Working with others

There are working groups out there that will take you in and teach you what they know, these training groups do exist, but are not easy to find, and they will be looking for honest committed people with an open mind and a desire to learn.

So, stay true to yourself, learn to keep your eyes and senses open, and I am sure they will appear, but when they do, "feal the ground" so to speak to make sure they are offering what you are looking for. I advise you to be careful who you listen to and work with, if they have given themselves, or want a grand name and expect to be treated in a grand way, just smile, and walk away. The main thing they will be interested in developing is their own ego and status.

Be prepared for a little wait if you want to join an existing group, the better ones tend to be a little secretive to protect members' anonymity and personal life, and selective because the wrong person can really disrupt the balance and flow of energies within a group, and that will ultimately affect the groups cohesion and even its continuation.

This is how a new person would normally be checked out before possibly being welcomed into a Greenheart group.

For the first few months, you may only knowingly meet one or two of the group's members, and will chat about quite mundane things. We are getting to know you and get a feel for what you are looking for.

If we like you a date will be agreed for you to start some basic training sessions, these will be regular sessions spread over at least six months to see if you are reliable, serious and committed about learning, and why you want to join the group.

You would then be invited to a meeting with all group members, we are seeing how you get on with everyone.

The next stage will involve a few months of training meetings to ensure you understand what you are getting into, and that you are reliable and committed to the group and its members.

If this goes well you would be invited to join us in a ritual or celebration; This would be something simple and you would not have a major part to play in it.

If during this time you show commitment, are consistent and true in your words and actions, you would probably be invited to become an active (stage one) member of the group.

There are normally three stages, or levels for full acceptance into a Greenheart group;

1. Personal dedication and commitment to the Green-heart path, its principals, and its members. Very similar to the one we looked at earlier, only more specific to the Greenheart way.

2. Acknowledgement by the group members of your reliability, commitment, and honesty to yourself and those who matter to you, and your desire to join the group.

3. Acceptance by the group of you as a member and fellow traveller on our journey, and by you of those who walk with you on this never-ending journey.

There is no set time frame for these different stages to be completed in, and some may not complete them through their choice or ours.

Acceptance to the group for membership is by agreement of all its current members.

There is no formal hierarchy within the group, all members are involved in all matters concerning the group.

The trust and respect between members of the group is something we earn through our actions, it is not expected or given because of a fancy title or robe.

Some people may be more experienced in certain areas than others, if they are, then it is their responsibility to pass on this knowledge to others within the group who want to learn those skills.

Back to the Beginning

Chapter 1

Questions and possibilities

Over the years I have read about, listened too, explored, been involved in, and experienced many variations of religious beliefs, paths, brotherhoods, callings, call them what you will, and I am always left with the same un-answered questions.

Everything must start somewhere, and we all have to accept that a "something" must have existed for everything else to start from.

I spent many years pondering those classic types of questions,

Where did we come from?

Why are we here?

Who is responsible?

I still do not, and have never met anyone who does have the answers. But I have met some who believe they have found their answers in a religious / spiritual belief system contained in a certain book, I am happy for them and would never try to tell anyone they are wrong.

So, the bottom line is what do **<u>you</u>** believe is possible or real?

Let us start at the beginning;

Where did the cosmos, the planets within it and the life upon them come from?

Where did it all start?

Where and how does life begin and end?

Does it begin and end? Or is it just recycled?

Was it all created by God/Goddess?

If it was then what were these God's and Goddess's doing for the millions of years before man existed?

Who or what created the Gods?

Did the gods create man, or did man create their God?

Is there something out there with a plan, if so, what?

They are all simple little questions that have been asked before, and I am sure will be asked again by better people than me, people that are "experts" in their respective fields of science, philosophy, and religion.

Another question for you to consider; could these "experts" be looking too hard for the answers they would like to find?

Some facts cannot be ignored i.e.

Energy and matter cannot be created or destroyed just redirected and reused, whether it is a baby being born, or the soil plants live in and feed on, nothing is new.

For example; they say oil and coal reserves are almost depleted, man did not make them, and cannot replace them, we merely became aware of their existence and then used and abused them.

As far as we know it is the plants and their energy that created the coal which we turn into fuel to power machinery that creates the items we want.

These different items will eventually fall into disuse, break down into their separate chemical parts and return to the earth, their origin, and so it goes on.

Life and death are interdependent in that way; a mountain stream may grow into a mighty river that ends its life by feeding the sea, which in turn creates rain to feed the mountain stream.

A mountain slowly breaks down and crumbles, filling the water-filled hollows below it, and creating fertile land for other life forms.

And whether the circle of life is water or land-based it follows the same never-ending cycle of life, death, and rebirth.

Plants rely on the organisms that break down dead matter, herbivores prey on the plants, carnivores prey on the herbivores, and the waste from all life forms is eventually recycled and re-used to create the future.

Something can be cremated, sealed in an airtight container, or buried deep within the Earth (as with radioactive waste) but nature will one day use it again, and we will not have any say as to when, or how, it is used.

I am not, and do not profess to be an expert in anything, and tend to go with a mixture of what I have been told, taught, common sense, and logic all confirmed when-ever possible, by actually doing what I am learning about. I then have the resulting experiences to think about and work with to make my final decision.

To move forward from here you need to accept and believe in the natural world, the real world, understand how it all fits together, know your place in it and understand how the jigsaw of life fits together and works.

Have you ever wondered how some animals seem to sense when danger is present, how they know if there is something "different" about an area and will not willingly go there?

It is readily accepted by many people that cats and dogs know when you are unwell, and they can sense or see a spirit / ghost, is this really possible?

Have you ever felt uneasy in a new or strange place,

or simply did not like a place or person for no apparent reason?

Have you ever met someone for the first time and straight away you are totally at ease with them and feel as if you have known them all your life?

Why and how does that happen?

I was taught that we are a part of nature, not above it, but part of it, and as such we have the same range of basic instincts as other animals. The only reason we cannot do what they do is because we have been told for so many generations that we cannot, or should not do these things, things that sadly most people have now forgotten how to do, but that natural instinct, and ability, are still within you, all you need to do is accept it is there, awaken it, and learn how to use it.

The challenge ahead for you now is to watch, listen, and learn from the life around you. You should study those life forms that are still an active part of nature, and understand how they use the natural energies for you to have any hope of learning to use them once again. To re-learn how to connect with those nonphysical unseen areas of life, those parts of nature we have been told do not exist, and have been taught to ignore.

Make time to take another look at things like dowsing, it has been proved to work, but the "experts" cannot agree how. Could it simply be the energy that is you, is detecting and connecting with the energy that is within what you are dowsing for?

Or could you be connecting to and drawing from the information and connective energy strands within the wyrd?

Does it really matter how you do it, or how it works, just learn to accept that it does.

Learn to relax, meditate, practice, develop and open those senses that will allow you to feel and be at one with nature again.

I found that when I stopped asking how and why things happen, and just accepted that they do, stopped asking how I could possibly draw on and use the Elemental Energies, and just accepted that I could. I found that not constantly trying to answer the unanswerable questions allowed me to relax and put me in a better frame of mind, and had more time, to look at and explore these different aspects and possibilities of life in a new way, only then did everything begin to fall into place for me.

It was around this time that I also began to meet new people with abilities and interests I had not really thought about. I had always accepted most of these things existed, but had never given them much thought or had the opportunity to discuss and explored them with like-minded people to see where, or if, these things fit into, or were already a part of the Greenheart way.

My initial training had given me an understanding of what the energies are, how they work, and their connection with every living thing, both physical and spiritual.

I had learnt that all I had to do was slowly acknowledge and accept each new possibility as and when the opportunity arose, with questions, thought, and meditation before cautiously exploring it.

So far, I have never changed or modified my core beliefs or what I do, new things just seem to fall into place within the natural circle of life.

When you have explored and accepted that everything comes from, and is still a part of those natural energies of life. Once you can accept, and know these basic things to be true, you do not **believe**, but you **know**, the same way you **know** the sun will appear in the morning.

We do not **believe** the sun will rise tomorrow, we do not **hope** it will, but we <u>**know**</u> it will, then you are ready to fully explore Greenheart and all it contains, discover and develop new skills, and find out who you truly are, or could be.

When you have reached your desired level within Greenheart there is no pressure or expectation of you to explore new possibilities the way I have. Many choose to live a simple, quiet, back to nature self-sustaining life.

Some people focus on, and work in, particular areas such as homeopathy, healing, and caring etc, etc. and some, like me continue exploring new areas and possibilities as we become aware of them. But whatever the chosen path is, it should always be travelled with nature as an anchor, companion and guide.

Chapter 2

My journey so far

The following is a progressive list of some of the different areas / things I have been made aware of, then explored, thought about, and worked at. Then after finding and understanding where and how they fit into nature I worked at accepting them, and luckily, they accepted me.

Some I have learnt about by simply listening to people I have been fortunate enough to come across, and then meditated on and explored what they said further when I had the time.

With others I have been lucky enough to speak to the people and they have told me what they do and why, then I have been guided through these (new to me) areas before (possibly) becoming involved in them.

Little tip for you, do not discount anything too quickly, some things are not always what they seem.

I will start at the beginning with the Old Ones, those Eternal Energies of Life, because understanding and accepting them has allowed everything else to fall into place and make sense. Their connection with nature was explained and shown to me from an early age, and because I grew up in the country and my family was part of a farming community everything I was told made perfect sense, and as I grew older I could see their words of wisdom in action as the seasons and the life within them came and went.

What we call the Old Ones is the origin and destination of everything. It was the "Big Bang" that started it and will be the "Black Hole" that ends it. But they do say that every end is also a new beginning.

Light passing through a diamond can leave a different colour and frequency from each face, think of that diamond as the Old Ones and each different colour and frequency as the Elemental Energies, we are all different but we are all part of the one.

The Old Ones are the origin of the Elemental Energies, and all life that is created from them. It is the Wyrd, that recyclable pool of energy and knowledge that flows from, and returns to the Old Ones.

Life forms may be created from the Elements but they are animated by the energy that all life draws on and returns to. It is that mix of memories and experiences we collect, and build during our life. When we connect with and draw on those energies it is the knowledge and memories held within the Wyrd that helps to build and shape our individual character and spirit, or what some may call our soul.

Being at one with the earth's energies; these are

the energies that can draw you to a place, or push you away. They can make a certain place feel "special" in some way such as your working area / circle. They may be seen and felt as ley lines, or be used when dowsing, scrying, or "seeing." They are the earthly conduit for the Wyrd, the earthly connection with other life forms, the past, and life on other plains. Even the "experts" admit there is an energy flowing within the earth, they just cannot agree on what it is, or what it does. The trick is to stop trying to explain what it is and just accept that it exists and that you are a part of it.

Once you can accept and understand these different areas within nature, and you know how to be at one with and use them, (I use the term <u>use</u> in the same way you would use a friend to help you with a task you could not complete on your own) and they can be blended and used to support each other. I will try to explain what I mean.

I will sometimes attain an **A S C** by **Meditating** on, and **Visualizing,** each step of opening my covenstead, the circle area that I have used for many years, and because of working there for so long I have developed a strong connection with the energies of that place. It does not matter where I am physically, mentally I am in my circle in the woods, I feel at one with that place and the energies that exist within and around it, at that moment I feel the same as physically being there. My personal energy, my essence, is at that place I know so well and feel a part of, and the energies of that place are there with me.

By using **Meditation** and **Visualization** I acknowledge and welcome each one in turn. I see them take form and can feel them join with me.

I feel the Old Ones at the centre, they are the origin of, still connected to, and holding everything else together.

I feel my personal energy sink its roots into the Earth beneath my feet and connect with its strength.

I feel the moisture (Water) in the air, and the blood flowing through my veins.

I feel the breeze on my face and the Air that fills my lungs.

I feel the warmth (Fire) of life within me and see the light of life around me.

I feel that spark of life (Ether) that created me and the life around me.

I see and feel those energies build and swirl around me until there is no them and me, only us.

This is when I become aware of what is around me, when I can be at one with, and draw on the energies of life that create and sustain us all.

This is when I am most able to connect with the unseen things that surround me, the things we are all a part of.

I blend and use them to help me in the task I have chosen to undertake at that time.

Visualization; I was taught there are two different types of Visualization, in the first you intentionally create a desired image to "see" the desired outcome of a ritual or need, as in a guided meditation where you intentionally create an image or scenario to explore an area for a certain reason.

I was told that if you only practise creating images then you will become very good at creating what you expect, or want to see, and these intentionally created images can blur or get in the way of what is really there.

For this reason, I was also taught to explore and connect with the life and energies around me, to accept and believe those unexpected images and snippets of information that appear in my mind or physically before me.

I was taught to trust those senses, feelings, and natural abilities that now seem to be frowned upon, hidden, or ignored in this modern world.

It was explained to me how the elemental energies do not always appear in the same way, or even look the same, sometimes they may be seen as part of the Element being welcomed i.e. you may feel a stone under your foot while doing Earth, see moisture on a leaf when welcoming Water, or an unexpected breeze may appear and be felt when acknowledging Air.

Or a misty area may form and grow around each element as it is acknowledged, there is no one and only way for them to join you, or their presence to be felt, but you will know when they are with you.

A tip that may help you "see things" when observing auras and scrying. When you have obtained the right frame of mind just relax your eyes, let them close a little and go out of focus, allow your natural senses to take over and just accept what you are "seeing".

Do not look for, or try to "see" something, just relax, and accept what you see, do not expect to immediately understand what you see, or for things to make sense straight away, the information may come in seemingly unrelated snippets that you have to separate and use to create a picture of meaningful information.

Think of a black bag that has had several different jigsaws (memories and time frames) emptied into it and then shaken. You do not know what pictures these jigsaws contain, and each time a piece is taken from that bag it may be from the same picture as last time, or they could be random pieces from different pictures, all you can do is stay calm, focused, and wait until you have enough similar pieces for the picture to make sense.

Do not be afraid to ask questions of that that

assorted bag of pieces, it may help you get pieces from the same jigsaw.

<u>Intentionally using energy for a specific purpose.</u> Some call this "magic," others think of it as prayer with a miracle as the outcome, and some say it is nothing more than positive thinking, but we will call it magic as it needs a short name rather than an in-depth description.

We (Greenheart) do this thing called magic very rarely, and only then after much deliberation on whether it is the only, or best way to achieve the required outcome.

Is it really necessary or could an acceptable result be achieved another way?

Let us say the problem is loneliness.

Is what you are planning the only option?

Is there a simpler way of achieving your goal?

Have you thought about joining a local group or club, or taking up a new hobby, something that will bring you into contact with new people?

Are you sure "magical" intervention is the only way?

If you decide this is the only way to achieve the required goal, what are you going to do to make it happen?

How are you going to do it?

When would you do it?

And what will you need?

Have you thought about, and are you aware of all the possible outcomes of what you are considering, and are you prepared to take responsibility for the outcome of this action?

Is everyone who may be affected by this aware of what you are about to do?

If you use magic to attract somebody then you could be taking them away from an existing relationship and those around them.

Are you prepared to take the responsibility for possibly breaking up a stable relationship / family and all the people that may be affected?

Look within yourself before drawing on and working with the Elements and Energies to full-fill your desire, the eventual costs of your actions could be more than you thought or are prepared to pay.

Doing magic involves raising energy, and energy should only be raised and used for positive reasons, with a known destination and end use in mind. It should never be done for fun or to simply show others you can do it, there is always a cost, are you prepared to pay it?

Magic is one of the few times when you need to

intentionally create and visualize a scenario and its end result i.e., if you send healing energy to something or somewhere you should know;

Who is it going to?

If it is just sent to an area in need, how do you know the right people have received it and will know what to do with it?

What are they going to do with it?

If the intended area and people do receive and know how to use it, what limitations have you put on its use?

What if they feel the right and necessary thing to do with it is different to what you had in mind?

What, and how, is it going to "heal"?

Magic, just like anything else has its limitations. If you call a builder to fix your home, they would need to know what is broken and then they will tell you if it is possible, the time scale, and the cost. There is always a cost.

How do you know the wrong person will not receive and use that energy for the wrong reasons?

You should always give the raised energy a destination and action, and you should monitor the situation through visualization and meditation until the desired action is complete.

Using plant's natural energies;

Some of the physical parts of plants have been used medicinally to cure and improve physical problems within animals and people for a very long time.

But as shown earlier the energies within these medicinal plants, and our spiritual association with certain other plants can also be used in an incense to affect our personal energy and frame of mind in a positive or negative way, this can be used to enhance a relaxing meditation, a celebration, or a ritual. But never forget that you are responsible for your creations, their use, and the outcome.

Energies of those who are no longer physically with us.

Within Greenheart we believe that when the physical shell we call the body has come to an end, the energy that helped it to grow, and animated it during its physical life, may return to the Wyrd or continue as a separate life form. But whatever it chooses to do their energy does not disappear, it is still there and should be remembered for what it was, and possibly still is.

Do not forget that energy is not, and cannot, be created or destroyed, it is re-cycled and re-used. The energy that we, and everything else draws on every day may carry the qualities and memories of long past life forms, memories that can give you details of a place you have never been to, or an insight into something you have never experienced.

I have a friend who is a very good, and highly thought of Spiritual Medium (something I knew very little about before we met) I discovered that for her to reach that level of ability she had studied and trained with two different mentors at a spiritual church for many years before we met. Her stories and experiences awakened my interest in her path, and her ability and knowledge inspired me to look deeper into what she done and how she did it, which then broadened my own vault of knowledge and experiences.

Exploring and embracing the spiritualist's knowledge and abilities have not changed my beliefs, it has enriched and expanded them, it has led me to develop and accept abilities I had not considered or used before.

Memories held in the land or a place.

Certain areas or places may hold the memories or presence of an old settlement, a traumatic event like a battle, the ancient memory of a forest of huge trees, or even the contact with life forms not of this world. I do not know how it work's I just accept that it does.

I have felt as if I was walking through a field of blood-soaked mud to later be told there was a brutal battle there many years ago.

I have walked through a barren landscape and seen the simple huts and animal pens that once stood in that place, and sensed the energy of the life that used to be there.

And yes, where possible I and others have checked out the historical records and details of some of these memories or visions, comparing them with the information I got at the time and found them to be true.

There have been places that I have been drawn to, encouraged to visit, and pushed towards. Then been made aware of something that simply wanted to be acknowledged so they could move on to join those they had shared their life with.

They, and their family did not know what had happened to them, they had simply disappeared, and the remaining solitary energy / spirit simply wanted someone to know the truth and acknowledge them so they could move on.

Calming energies trapped within a place or building.

As I said earlier, I have become involved in a few things by accident, this is my first step into one of those accidents.

I was asked by a spiritualist medium if I would accompany them to a house that had strange noises and things happening. These "strange things" were making the mother uneasy and frightening the children at night.

The medium had been asked if she would "clear" the house of "ghosts and negative energies" but did not want to go on her own. Now I had been taught, and had always accepted, that "ghosts" and "spirits" existed, but had never had the reason or opportunity to explore why they do what they are supposed to do, but I had always been curious to know more about these spirits / energies, how and why do they interact with the physical world? and can they really be negative or dangerous?

So naturally I jumped at the chance.

This is an account of my first foray into an area of past lives, ghosts, and spirits. My first attempt to intentionally try to connect with and calm a "troubled spirit."

I have changed the names of the people and places involved to protect their privacy.

House by a churchyard.

Jane, a spiritualist medium, asked me to accompany her to a village near Ely to try and help a young family that had recently moved into a new house by a church. They had two boys aged three and five who were not sleeping properly because of unexplained noises during the night i.e. sobbing sounds and doors and draws opening and closing. The mother also felt so uncomfortable in her own bedroom that she did not like going in there, and some evenings there was a burning smell on the landing outside her room and at the top of the stairs. She and her husband thought it was all connected to the graveyard next to their house.

The husband worked long hours and was concerned about his family but was not as aware as his wife as to what was happening. I requested the children not to be there during the visit, or be told about anything that went on while I was there.

After spending some time walking around the house, "opening up" and connecting to the energies / spirits, I became aware of a woman in her twenties and her young son who had both died in a house fire many years before. I was told their current house was built on virgin land that had no record of any previous dwellings. I discussed my findings with Jane, and we then went back to the master bedroom to meditate with the hope of gaining more detail, but the feeling in the upper storey of the house was now becoming "less friendly" and Jane went back downstairs to sit with the mother.

I soon became aware of a voice in my head telling me of a fire in the family's previous house where a woman had died trying to save her young son. After the fire the empty shell of this house was just left empty for many years leaving the spirit of the mother and her son on their own waiting for someone to come for them. For all those years her and her son were alone until the house was eventually done up and a newly married couple moved in. Eventually the newly-weds had a son, which pleased the spirit mother as her son had a friend.

When her son's friend moved, they both went with him.

Then another child joined them (his younger brother) and the older boy was making new friends at school and no longer wanted to play with his spirit friend.

So, her son became unhappy because his friend stopped playing with him, and his mother was angry because her son was unhappy.

I went downstairs and asked where the couple had lived before and was told it was an old flint-built place that had been gutted by fire years ago, and they had bought it from the builder who had done it up.

Both their sons had been born there but they needed more room and moved when the youngest was still a baby. The husband then said it was a really nice little place with a good feel about it and they did not really want to go, but needed more room for the growing family.

I asked when the problems started, and they said it was soon after their oldest started the local school and made some new friends.

At this point, I told them what I had found and explained it was only a mother trying to make her child happy. Somehow, I knew we could free the mother and child from their sadness and make the couple's house a happier place to live.

I decided to create an incense mixture to give the mother and her son peace by showing them a better place to be. I also cleansed the area for the current family.

To create that incense I used;

Lavender, Sweet laurel, Valerian, Hawthorn bloom and Elder Flower plus a grass seed head, then added some Myrrh and Drammer to the mix, this was burnt in the master bedroom.

While this was burning, I spoke to the troubled mother and her son about the life they had before the fire, and about her husband who was waiting for her and his son to join him.

I then sat on the edge of the bed and visualised the mother and her son returning to their place in time, and their waiting family. I watched them slowly fade as they went back to their husband / father. I then smeared a little Patchouli oil around the children's bedroom doors and windows, and at the top of the stairs as a sensual lift for the family. I finally joined Jane and the mother downstairs.

Before we left, I asked the mother to go upstairs to the bedrooms and she was surprised to find not only had the unpleasant smell had gone, but she felt more relaxed than she had for a long time.

Jane received a call the following week to say the two boys were now sleeping through the night, the noises and smells had all gone, and to thank us for what we did.

That was my first "spirit calming" visit which took place in the early 1990s. There have been many more since then, but no two have ever been the same in problem or outcome.

And to answer your question, yes, I have been to some that were more challenging than others. Places where once things got underway some of the people with me refused to stay in the room, or even the immediate area while I continued doing what was needed.

I suggest you work on your personal protection energy before delving into this sort of thing, and please be careful how you approach, and work with these unknown energies.

And I ask you to treat these life forms, spirits, beings from another realm, call them what you will with consideration and respect. Do not contact them for your amusement or to prove to others you can, and please do not try to annoy them just to get a reaction that can be seen on a piece of equipment.

Always remember their final actions may not have the same restrictions and limitations as the physical world we live in.

Energies from other worlds. I was taught, and have always accepted there is life on other worlds. You would have to be a very blinkered person to think that the Earth is the only planet with sentient life, and that the human animal is the most advanced life form not only on this planet but in the cosmos.

As any life form in the cosmos will be created from the same elemental ingredients as the earth and the life upon, and everything living thing is animated by the same energy, why shouldn't we be able to feel a connection to, and be aware of life on other worlds?

Being aware of and connecting with an otherworldly energy / lifeform is another area I stumbled into after meeting a married couple at a small monthly gathering where like-minded people can, and do, just sit and discuss their thoughts and interests on a wide range of topics. One of the things talked about that evening was UFOs and aliens, and before the night was over, I had been invited to join a few people on a visit to Rendlesham forest, where in the early 1980s there was a well-documented sighting by military personnel of an unexplained craft and associated lights.

We arrived at Rendlesham forest in the early evening when the hustle of the day was coming to an end. I had always taken for granted that life existed on other planets but I had never knowingly sensed or connected with any other worldly beings or energies, and it was a strange sensation for me to intentionally go and look for them.

After spending a little time clearing our thoughts in preparation for what we were about to do, we then spent about three hours just slowly following the signposted UFO Trail (yes there is an official trail) we slowly walked around the perimeter of the military base (it is no longer operational) and other areas of the woodland just to "see" what is there, and between us we discovered there was a lot more than just alien energies in the area.

I had no prior knowledge of that area and had never been to Rendlesham before, but I knew where the lights had been seen, where the ship had come down, why they had visited, and still continue to visit that area.

Since that first visit and experience at Rendlesham, I became aware that this was not my first encounter with otherworldly energies / lifeforms. I now know and accept that all life forms throughout the cosmos are part of, and work with, the same energy source as we do.

I had it confirmed to me that night that energy is energy, and the earth could hold the memories of previous events of both humans and aliens.

That evening, I also became aware there are some very old, and very strong earth energies in that area that have nothing to do with other worldly life forms.

Words and Actions

Chapter 1

Stop and look within.

This book is almost finished, but your path may have just begun, so I will try to leave you with a few tips and things to consider;

As I said at the start of this book, Greenheart is a simple Nature-based path of action more than words, and we, Greenheart people, prefer face-to-face discussions and training so questions can be asked, answers explained, and new people are able to explore and experience things in a safe controlled environment. But I accept the best I can hope for with this book is to awaken your interest in things you may not have considered or even been aware of before.

The following seven items are simple, but important little things that can make all the difference to the outcome of connecting to, and being at one with, nature and all that is part of it.

1; Watch how nature works and lives;

Learn from it, see how it all fits together and works as one, remember that you are trying to connect with life's natural energies and experience all they have to offer, they are not waiting for you to join them.

They are not aware of your existence or trying to gain you as a friend so you must play by their rules, and do not expect them to change these rules just to suit you.

Always remember that somewhere in the future, you, and everything else, will return to where it came from, those natural elemental energies, and everything will be used once again to create something new.

2; Take the time to experience the different parts of nature.

Stand barefoot on the earth and feel its energy flow up into your body and strengthen your physical self.

Be aware of a single raindrop as it lands on your skin, then feel it slowly roll down and awaken your senses.

Allow a warm summer breeze to flow into, and through you, feel it blow away all the dross and problems of everyday life.

Feel that bright heat of the sun as it warms not just your outer body, but also enlivens and invigorates the inner you.

Stand quietly in nature and be aware of all the

different life forms around you, think about where they came from, that spark of life that entered a seed to begin an uncertain journey, and all that is needed for their journey to continue.

Never forget that we also started from a seed and have an uncertain journey in front of us.

Open yourself to a full moon and feel it awaken your inner self and senses. Experience the different stages of the moon, it has enough power to affect the tides and plant growth, and it most certainly affects us as well.

Be aware of the moon phases and keep notes on how you feel at those different stages, you may notice a pattern, a connection with a full or dark moon that you can use to help plan the best time for things you want to do.

When being at one with and experiencing the elements, expose as much skin as you feel comfortable with, you must accept, understand, and be at one with something before you can expect to be fully accepted as part of it.

You may now have feelings of self-conscious panic coursing through your mind i.e. I am too out of shape, old, wrinkly, hairy, overweight, scrawny, etc. etc. these thoughts and fears have been created by modern society stereotypes and expectations, they are not relevant in the real / natural world.

A twenty-year-old tree may have a pretty shape and smooth bark, but it is the gnarly five-hundred-year-old tree that life turns to for protection and shelter, and you will seek the wisdom and knowledge of the weathered old person who lives on the edge of society, not the pretty youngster down the pub.

3; Be true to yourself.

Anger, pride and ego will consume time and energy but give you nothing in return, and self-doubt will limit your ability to experience and enjoy all this life has to offer.

Be honest with yourself about yourself. You do not have to change anything just accept who you are, and be aware of how you treat others.

4; Do not "cherry-pick" the interesting bits of life.

These "interesting" bits are part of and supported by the "boring" bits, I have met some of the most interesting people while exploring the boring bits.

Do not forget that everything is connected and learning any new skill should be done in a certain order, just doing the "interesting" bits can affect your final goal, desired ability, or even safety.

Example; Would you learn to dive before you learnt to swim?

Or would you go for a swim before checking what is in the water?

5; Greenheart is not a belief but a Knowing and way of life.

Some people want a path or belief system where they can dip in and out depending on how they feel and what they are doing, they want to be part of something that allows them to do things with like-minded people that gives them a warm fuzzy feeling of doing their bit in saving the world.

In Greenheart we try to acknowledge, be aware of, and work with nature on a daily basis, not only when it is convenient for us. We do not do this to save the world, the earth and life upon it existed for millions of years before humans appeared and will continue long after humans have gone.

We do this because we want to retain the worlds' ability to support life as we know it, the life we are a part of.

We want to continue enjoying the life and abilities we possess to their fullest.

6; Do not judge others by your ideals.

Try to accept and love others for who they are and they may do the same for you.

7; Your most treasured possession should be your body.

Your greatest gift is your life.

Look after the first, enjoy the second and your time here can be wonderful.

I want to remind you that the words I have used in the rituals are not set in stone, and can / should be changed if they do not "feel right" or fit the reason for their use.

Do not forget that you are not talking to a superior being of some kind, but to the inner you.

These words and statements should be said with meaning and intention, they should speak to the energies within you, that part of you that contains those otherworldly abilities that can enhance the life you have been given, so please give any new words some thought, try to make them" flow" with a rhythm and continuation that fits the actions, meaning, and desired outcome of the ritual etc.

Do not think of meditation, ritual, and visualization as separate items, that are used at different times for different reasons. Meditation can help you achieve an A.S.C. (Altered State of Consciousness) a frame of mind where you can release and use your personal energy to explore and connect with the non-physical life, we are a part of, it allows us to be aware of and connect with the unseen life around us.

Achieving and maintaining an A.S.C. during a ritual can help you reach a whole new level of connection, experience, and meaning, and with regular practice you can learn how to slip between the physical and non-physical worlds with a simple thought and gesture, to connect and disconnect as needed.

Chapter 2

Slow down to learn

I have been walking this path for over sixty years now, and have been lucky enough to learn and experience things at a trickle, almost one thing at a time. I was fortunate to spend my childhood in the country and grow up surrounded by nature. I experienced the seasons come and go, and watched the energies give and take life. I experienced the turning of the wheel and was shown how life depends on death and how death, in turn, is the beginning of life. I was not only taught how the wheel of life turns but also my part within it.

Within these pages I have tried to show you how we in Greenheart connect, and work, with Nature's Elemental Energies of Life. I have done this to try and keep a promise I made many years ago, a promise to pass on not only what I was taught at the beginning of my journey, but what I have learnt along the way.

For this reason, I have included the next piece to encourage you to take it slowly, think about, explore, and master, each step before rushing to the next.

Walk don't run

I'm the grain of the harvest, the oak of the forest
The lives of a deer, bird and fish I have seen

The trials of life and their companion sorrow
Have taken me back many times to the green

The knowledge of time, the magic of nature
Were shown to me as each life began
My first lives, those others, I did not take notice
But now I walk, then I ran

The deer, bird and fish think not of tomorrow
Nor do they worry about the past
The wolf and the hawk do not see sorrow
In the death of their food, or if it's their last

All these are but steps in the stages of life
The victim, the victor, who knows what is right
Each life being lived, by what has to be done
No thought hardly given to adults or young

In this life I see the young and the old
The past and the present, what the future may hold
I listen to nature, heed the knowledge of time
With their help I've created this life of mine

I come from the past, a journey of learning
A long winding journey of questions and yearning
I've learnt on this journey how life's magic is
missed
I've studied the knowledge, I now know it exists

But my time is not over, I've more lives to live
More senses to awaken, more knowledge to give
More lessons to learn, the futures not done

So, I pass on this message, walk, don't run.

Chapter 3

Before Greenheart had a name.

At the beginning of my journey along this path it was explained to me how people have pondered on, and talked about, the origin and power of life, and why they have probably done this since humans first walked the Earth, and how they continue to speculate on life's physical creation and the energy that animates that creation. The energy we originate from, and will always remain a part of.

Where did everything come from, where does the beginning begin, where, when, and how does it end, or does it?

Does life end, enter another level / stage, or just start again?

It is also a fairly safe bet that from the beginning of that search for an answer, explanation or reason for our existence, they looked for a Creator, a God, an Omnipotent being to take the responsibility of answering these questions.

They looked to it for guidance, they wanted it to protect them in this life, and the next, they wanted something to take responsibility.

But a few of these searchers took a different path and looked at the natural world around them, they listened to what it was saying, acknowledged what it said, and learnt from what they saw, they learnt how to be at one with, and experience the powers of life for themselves.

Myth, lore and legend may tell how some have seen this power or energy in visions, learnt of the wheel of life, and understood how it turns. But these stories do not tell you how this was achieved, they do not tell of the time and commitment of these dedicated few.

They watched the wheel of life, they saw what it was and understood how it turns.

They listened to nature, heard what it said and learnt from what they heard.

They understood where life came from, where it went, and how it returned.

They listened to this age-old energy of life and learnt how it flowed.

They learnt how to be as one with this flow, and the knowledge it contains.

They learned of nature's power, how to use it, and the possible cost of its use.

They watched life grow old and die, only to see it return new and fresh once again.

They became one with their surroundings and learnt from that experience.

These mystics, these heroes, these saviours, were sometimes uncertain what their actions would cost them, but they carried them out just the same.

According to some myths and legends their actions may have saved a loved one, a King or a country, or monsters and evil may have been banished.

These things were done for love, duty and honour, not personal gain or fame.

These deeds were done by a human, not a God.

They had gained the strength and courage to complete their task, but told very few where that inner strength came from or how to draw on it.

Some of these people, these heroes, are remembered in story and song, in tales that tell of the deeds that were done, but these tales rarely suggest where they got the power to carry out these actions.

Their stories were polished each time they were told. Gods and magical spirits were created to explain how the challenge was completed.

These stories weren't written by the people, the heroes who vanquished the evil whatever it was, or even by those who were there when the deed was done.

But by those who heard of what happened and felt others should now of the brave deed long after the kingdom was saved from the evil monster, savage beast, etc, etc.

So the tellers could only tell of what they heard, not what they saw, and they recounted the tale to inform and entertain those listening.

They polished the story to make it shine and boost their reputation as a story teller, it may well have been how they made a living.

But only those involved, the heroes that completed the task knew the power they worked with and where it came from, they knew it existed before words, names, temples and Gods.

It has been, and still is, called many things, but it needs no name.

It has been given many bodies and faces, but it has no form.

It was at the beginning before things began, and at every step of creation since.

When the ingredients of life are mixed it is there, but it plays no part in the success of the outcome, it just makes life possible.

It has no desire or need for your worship, and has no use for physical offerings and gifts.

It has no use for temples, and any penance and gifts go unnoticed.

It does not care what you call it, or where you come from.

It cares not what we do with the gifts we possess, they are ours to use, abuse, or ignore.

Those gifts, abilities, and us, will all return to that constant flow of energy when our time is over.

I'm not saying this is fact, this is how it was explained and taught to me, and this is how things are in my world, in the real world that is nature.

Chapter 4

A thought to leave you with

I realise what I have told you within these pages may be a little more than you were expecting, or able to take in, so I end this book with a short story that may give you something to think about while you decide where to go from here.

The colours of life

A class of primary school children from a big city were visiting a retirement home with Christmas gifts for the residents. After a while one of the children wandered over to this very old resident sitting quietly in an armchair looking out of the window.

They had a friendly smiling face with skin the colour and texture of weathered leather, and the small child asked; "why do all the trees and flowers look so grey and sad?"

The old person turned and looked at the child, then with a smile asked if they would like to hear the story their grandparents had told them about the colours of life.

The child excitedly said yes and called the others, and so the children sat down in a circle on the floor and the story began.

Many years ago, all the different types of life lived by listening to, and helping each other. Their lives, and what they needed to live, fitted together just like pieces in a jigsaw, each knowing that they, and life itself would be incomplete without all the other pieces.

Life may not have been easy but it flowed smoothly through the seasons with everything having what it needed to enjoy their time here.

There were also a few beings in this land that were hard to describe, some called them gods, others called them spirits. Granddad said people called them many different things, but they did not seem to mind what they were called as long as you treated the life around them and the land with respect.

But it seems these beings may also have played an important part in the circle of life itself by keeping an eye on things, and making sure the life around them had the right colours and smells in the right places at the right times.

Nobody questioned their existence they were just accepted as part of life. Why should anybody doubt them? The sun rose in the morning, new life came from old and the seasons smoothly turned the wheel of life, and nobody questioned that either!

The peculiar thing about this land was how the inhabitants interacted.

You see the trees did not just bloom, hope for the best then bear fruit, oh no. In this land the North wind would tell the trees when the last frost of winter had been scattered so they would know it was safe to open their buds, and the birds would tell the clouds when the earth was getting dry.

Now the humans would listen in on these conversations and help things along the best they could, nothing very exciting, they cleared the rubbish from the ground, made sure the bees had a safe home during winter, helped protect young plants and animals, and gathered and stored the harvest for the benefit of not only themselves, but all life around them during the cold lean times.

That does not mean the different creatures were all friends. This was not a happy ever-after place of milk and honey with wolves gently stroking rabbits. Everything knew that something had to die for another to live, it was a simple fact they all accepted as a natural part of life. All the inhabitants had to do their bit, nothing in life is for free.

For many generations, this all worked well for everything concerned. Good and bad bits balanced out and life rolled along nicely with everything doing its bit to keep the jigsaw fitting tightly together for the benefit of all. Everything had food, shelter, and a tomorrow. The wheel of life had a strong axle and it turned with a purpose. What more could anything ask for?

But what of the strange mystical beings that nobody knew much about? They were never seen to eat, drink or sleep and were always dressed in beautifully coloured robes. Nobody ever saw them arrive or leave anywhere, they were just there watching, or not if you know what I mean.

According to the stories they were never actually seen doing anything either, but if a house was being built, crops harvested or a baby was born and one of them was there, you knew things would be OK.

That is how life rolled along for many generations until one of the humans decided they could not be bothered to "do their bit." Why should they?

The trees would bear fruit and chickens lay eggs whether they helped them or not, which of course was true.

The fruit was not as tasty, but you could eat it, and they put the chickens in cages because it made the eggs easier to collect.

The chickens did not like being caged and their food was not as good, but they were never asked for their opinion.

These "time-saving" ideas spread to other humans. It made their lives easier they said, and gave them more time to do other more worthwhile things they said. Granddad did not say what these other worthwhile things were, but they must have been really good?

Well, all these new ideas put things out of balance, greed and power went hand in hand with laziness and pride until the humans just stopped listening to the world around them altogether.

There was no place for magic and mystery in their new way of life. To them the jigsaw no longer mattered so the missing pieces were not even noticed!

While all these changes were taking place the watchers just sat in the distance. They did not interfere as the pieces of the jigsaw continued to slip away, the skies became black with smoke, lush green forests became empty barren soil and blossoms lost their scent.

It is said that as the colours slowly drained from the land it also drained from them, until one day these beings with their bright swirling robes were gone.

My old granddad said he was told that when humans can be bothered to look for the missing pieces of the jigsaw and begin to put it back together, the colours may start to come back.

The old weathered resident ended their story by saying; so, I ask you all to help look after the world around you and listen carefully to what it is saying. You never know, you might hear a piece of the jigsaw calling, and if the colours come back into your garden the watchers may be able to spread it out to your neighbours and then slowly into the rest of the world.

The children sat quietly for a while, then a buzz of excitement started to build within the youngsters before finally exploding in a torrent of questions, until finally they left the room excitedly making plans to bring the colours back to the world.

I end this story with a question for you;

Are you content to be like that old person who sits comfortably in their chair looking through a window at the world outside, who sometimes remembers and retells the stories of how things once were and could be again?

Or are you one of the children determined to do all you can to bring the colours back into our world?

If I have left you with more questions than answers, please feel free to use this contact and I will be happy to help you look for an answer to your question.

lesliehartrudd@gmail.com

Take care, relax, and enjoy your journey on this path with no end.

Printed in Dunstable, United Kingdom

78062146R00107